His Majesty, the Queen

by

Frank Marino

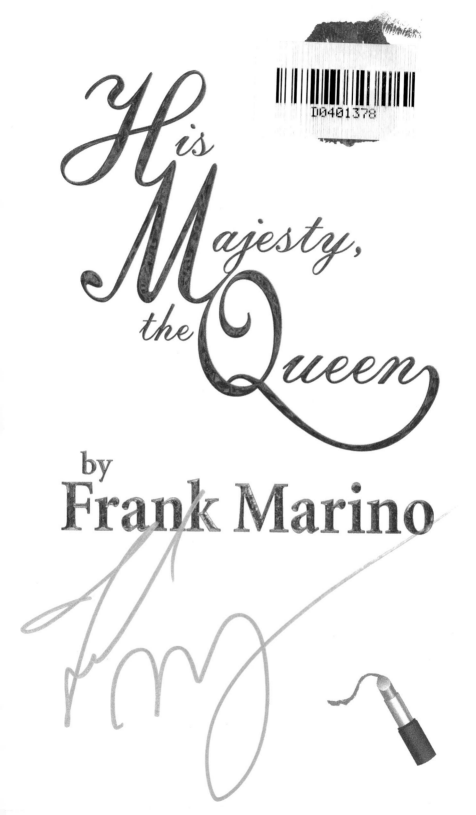

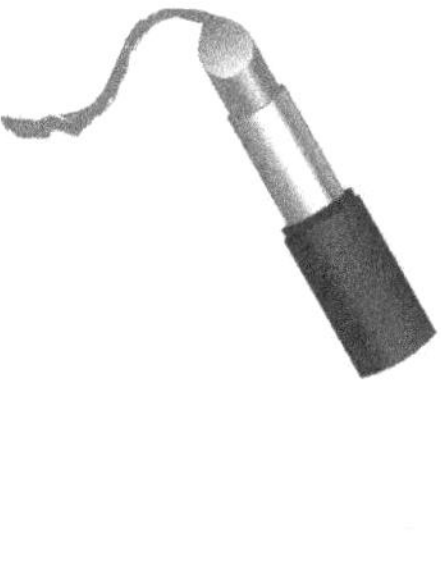

His Majesty, the Queen
(An Autobiography)

Owned and Published by:
Frank Marino Enterprises
9041 Sandy Shores Drive
Las Vegas, NV 89117
702-363-5768

ISBN-13: 978-0692284377
ISBN-10: 0692284370

Photo Credits: Tim Davis, Rocky Thies, Tanner Cole, Susan J. Meyer.
All others from the Frank Marino collection.

Library of Congress Catalog Card Number: 96-077477
First MSW hardcover printing January 1997.
10 9 8 7 6 5 4 3 2 1

For more information address:
Frank Marino Enterprises,
9041 Sandy Shores Drive,
Las Vegas, NV 89117

A Dream Come True. One Boy, One Girl, One Heart, Beating for Two

Nightly after my show in **Las Vegas**, people come up to me and ask me all kinds of questions. The ones I recall being asked most frequently are: "Who does your **hair**?" "Who does your **makeup**?" However, most often I'm asked, "Where did you get those beautiful **gowns**?"

I decided it would just be easier to answer all their questions at once. That is my purpose for writing this book.

Right off the bat, let me start by saying, "I am a **female impersonator**!" This is a person who dresses in drag for entertainment purposes only or, of course, for large sums of **cash**. "Therefore, I rarely dress up at home." Just kidding!

I am often mistaken for either a **transvestite**, which by definition is a straight man dressed in women's clothing for sexual pleasure, or a **transsexual**, which is, for lack of better words, a woman trapped in a man's body who has surgery to change her sex. "I've always believed that if God wanted me to be a woman, He would have given me the **ten grand** for the operation." For me, **drag** is just show time!

So, with the swish of my hips and a stroke of a makeup brush, I became a major success in a complicated and controversial job market. I'm a businessman by day and a female **superstar** by night. The reality may be that I am a man, but the illusion is that I am a woman!

With the whole world at my fingertips, I still keep reaching for me.

For the first time ever, I tell it all and share my most intimate thoughts and feelings. My life thus far has just been your typical **All American Story**… with a **twist**!

Once Upon a Time

I dreamed of writing
"A Fairy Tale!"
Now, my dream has come true! Let us step through the looking glass together, as we enter the kingdom of:

His Majesty, the Queen.
The Frank Marino Story

Dedication

A single real friend is a treasure worth more than gold or precious stones. Money can buy many things, good or evil. But all the wealth in the world cannot buy a friend, or pay for the loss of one! This book is dedicated to all the great performers in the past that we have sadly lost to AIDS. To those who have paved the way for me to become who I am today! AIDS is a very strong and powerful disease, but, we as the Human Race are stronger and can defeat it!

Keep the faith!

~ Frank Marino

Acknowledgments:

My deepest thanks to:

God - Without you there would be nothing.

Mom and Dad - I'll always love you and will never, ever forget you.

Aunt Sarah – For becoming my mother when I didn't have one.

Lucille – For always being there when I need you.

Alex (Shannon) – For accepting me for me and making a real difference in my life.

Russ – For being a true friend and doing things others wouldn't have.

Mary – I'm so glad I found you and you let me be a part of your life.

Norbert Aleman – Now we both know what made the show so successful.

Greg Kramer – For being the first person to show the world who Frank Marino is.

Lou & Anthony Paciocco – For taking a chance on a then-unknown 20-year-old.

The Divas Cast – For letting me share the spotlight with you guys.

Diana Ross – For years of inspiration.

Joan Rivers – For without you, I would have no career.

The Riviera Hotel – For giving me my first home in Las Vegas.

The LINQ – For giving me my present home in Las Vegas

Some of the names in this book have been changed to protect the innocent.

Although, I really don't think it will help!

Table of Contents

The price of beauty depends on which department store you shop in.

1

Let's Face It!

I've always felt that organization is the key to being successful at whatever it is you're trying to do. Believe me, if I'm going to make this dark-haired Italian boy look like a fair-skinned blonde woman, I'd better be organized.

The vanity in my dressing room is set up with every tube and jar of makeup in an exact location. **I always put my brushes and creams to my left and my shadows and powders to my right, allowing enough room to place my lighted mirror directly in front of me.** I strongly believe that correctly positioning the tools of my trade is just as critical as the actual application itself.

Boy oh boy, do I have my work cut out for me.

Before I begin on my face, I do some odds and ends. The first thing I do after entering my dressing room is dim the lights. Once the lights are lowered, I turn on some soft music, pour myself a glass of juice, and shed off all my boy clothes that I have worn that day. I then put on my white terry cloth robe and turn on the vaporizer as I apply a hot washcloth to my face. **At this point I lean forward into the gentle mist and allow my mind to dispose of all the unnecessary, unfinished business of the day.** The steam, aided by the hot washcloth, helps to smooth and prepare my skin for all I am about to instill upon it. Breathing and relaxing are half of what it's all about. The transformation is both physical as well as mental. **Becoming a goddess is as much a state of mind as a look.**

Once I'm completely relaxed, I saturate my face and neck with moisturizer. This not only softens my skin but acts as an undercoat so that all my makeup will go on smoothly.

I begin the process by applying moustache wax on my eyebrows. This helps to eradicate them on a temporary basis since I absolutely refuse to pluck or shave them.

From there, it's onto the nose putty. I use the putty to hide any and all traces of sideburns. This actually makes them invisible, as if they were a part of my skin.

Next, I apply (the drag queen's dream) a coat of Max Factor pan stick. I stipple my entire face with a wet sponge to blend all the areas together.

When the base makeup is completely even and there are no tell-tale lines showing, I apply a layer of translucent facial powder. I use a medium peach tone to give

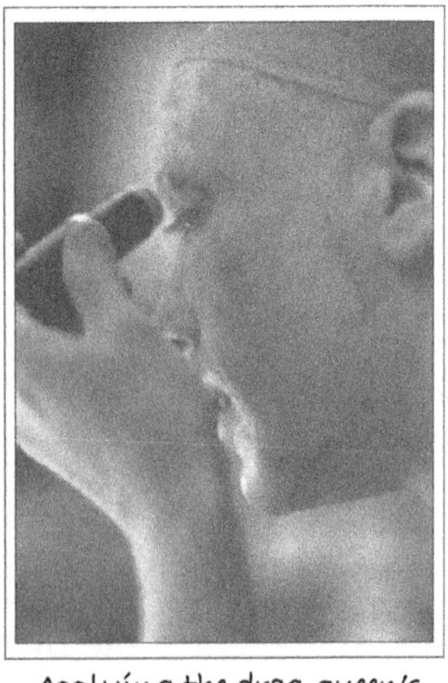

Applying the drag queen's dream Max Factor pan stick.

Creating an eyebrow with an angled brush.

me a soft apricot glow. The powder gives my whole face a beautiful matte finish.

One sure thing you need to look out for is that awful line around your neck where your base coat ends and your natural skin color begins. The end result of that mistake is you look like you've recently had a head transplant. That's one of the reasons I always go all the way down to my shoulders with the makeup in order to make it all blend properly.

This is also a great trick for women who want their breasts to appear larger than they really are. If I'm wearing a low cut dress, I even put makeup on my chest. I will contour the center with a dark brown powder and place a lighter colored powder over where the breasts would be. This gives the illusion of cleavage.

At this point, I lean back and stare at the blank face in the mirror. There is no trace of gender left whatsoever. I have now created a blank canvas with which to work.

I begin by drawing on my eyebrows. Believe it or not, the eyebrows play the most important part of the face. You have to know the angle and thickness of each character you portray. It would be impossible to portray bushy eye-browed Brooke Shields with pencil thin eyebrows. To do

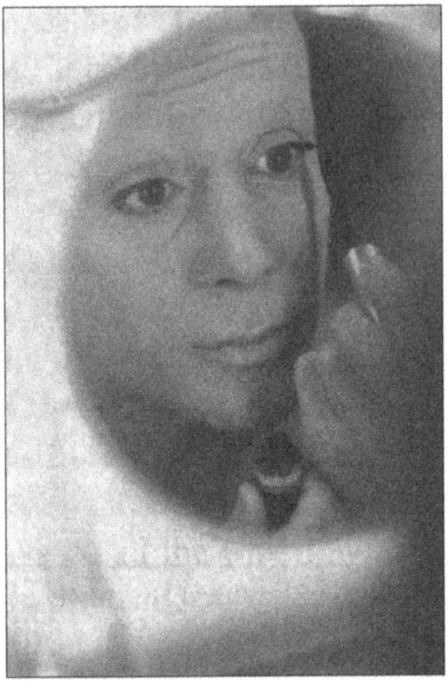

Never smudge, never smear, Adrien Arpel mascara is here.

this, I use an angle brush to achieve the perfect arch.

It is also vital to use the correct colors. I can't stand to see a beautiful blonde with black eyebrows. For Joan Rivers I use a brownish color called brawn. I then sweep over it with an orange-rust color called teaberry. This gives it a fabulous auburn hue.

The next step is the eyelashes. I have always preferred Adrien Arpel Mascara. By trial and error I have discovered it to be the best, as it doesn't smudge or clump together on my lashes. If I put mascara on my lower lashes, that's where I'd like it to stay. **I don't want to look in the mirror and see dozens of little dots on my cheekbones.**

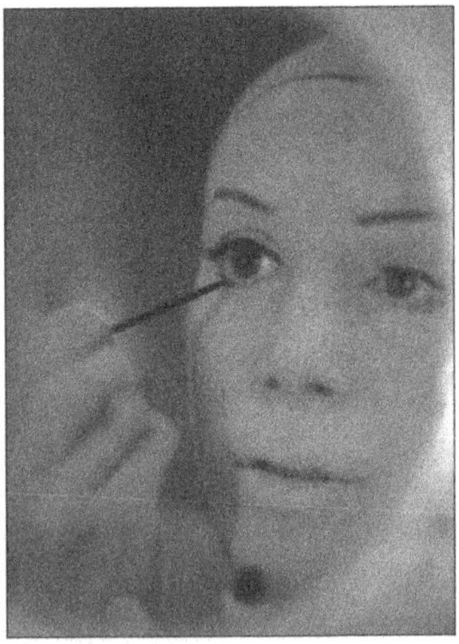

You must keep a steady hand when applying Cover Girl liquid eyeliner. (If I miss, I'll look like KISS.)

Now, when it comes down to eyeliner, believe it or not, Cover Girl deep black works best for me. As far back as I can remember, Cover Girl eyeliner has been my favorite.

The applicator brush is just the right size to get a smooth line with just one stroke and the best part is that it dries almost immediately, which is what you look for in a liquid eyeliner.

As for the eye shadows and blushes, I use Sebastian because they make the most incredible color line ever available. **There is a perfect shade for every gown I have ever worn!** Believe me when I say I have tried them all. I have! With Sebastian, the choices are endless. They are always keeping up with the times and the biggest plus is that you can get them at almost every beauty salon.

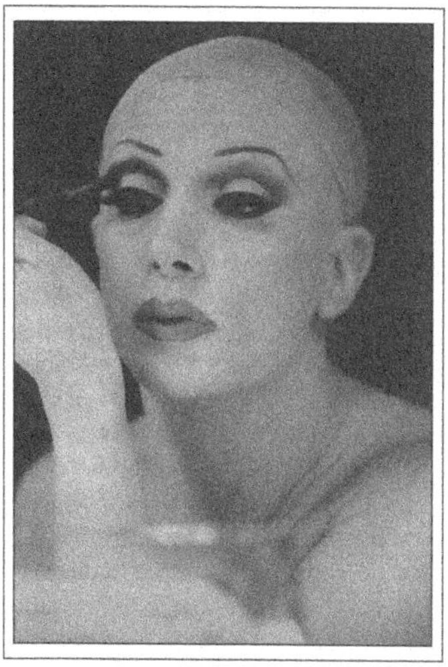

Creating drama with my eyes has always been my specialty.

I start my eyes by putting bone eye shadow over my entire lid. I then use iron ore red to make a crease from the nose to the outer eye. This gives them a very dramatic, defined look which is great for the stage. I finish the look by blending it all together with some playful peach. I then put on false eyelashes so that I can achieve the thickest, lushest lashes possible. **Nothing beats a gorgeous set of eyes!**

Once I am satisfied with my eyes, I concentrate on my lips. I outline the shape of the lip with a dark red lip liner which allows me a little bit of room to cheat if I have to. I can make my lips appear either fuller or thinner, depending on the thickness of the dark red outline. When I'm impersonating Joan Rivers, I use Chanel #70 for the blood-

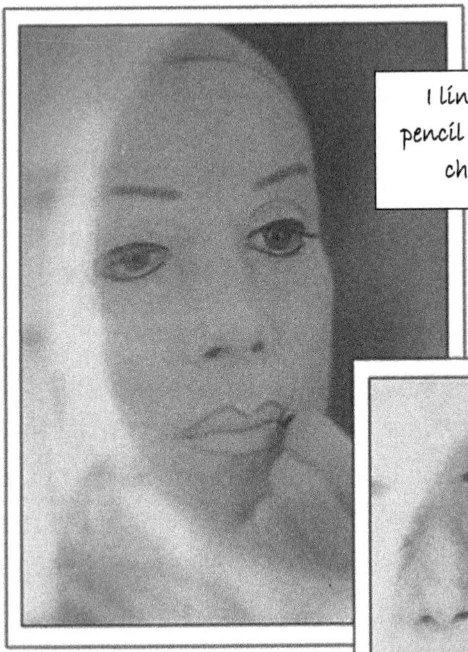

I line my lips with a deep red pencil to get the exact shape of the character I'm portraying.

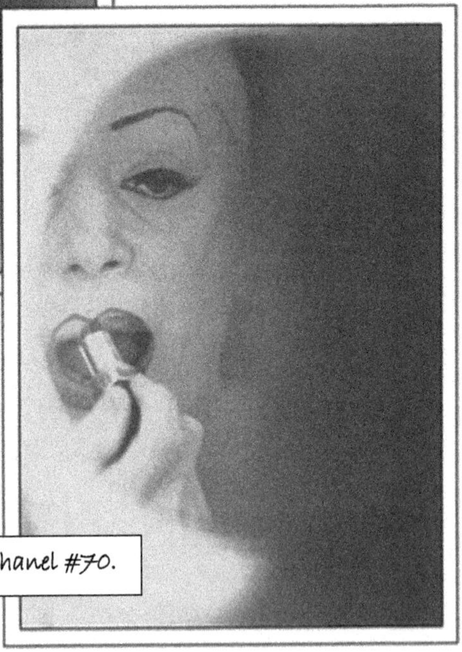

My favorite lipstick color is Chanel #70.

red look that she has. Over that, I usually apply Flory Roberts Raha red lip gloss, which adds the perfect shine. The lip liner I've used helps prevent the lip gloss from running over or under my lips to my teeth. **There's nothing worse than having a perfect face and red teeth.**

Rosy red cheeks make a girl look healthy.

The next step for me is to take a little white coral, stoplight orange and ribbon pink and mix them all together to give my cheeks that rosy red look you get when you go outside in the dead of winter.

When all the colors seem to be in the right place, I do a thing called sharpening the jawline. I take my flat blush brush and the same dark powder I used on my chest and draw a thin line from under my ear to my chin and up to my other ear. This gives a very defined look between my face and my neck.

This is a great trick if one needs to get rid of a double chin.

As for the makeup brushes I've been talking about, **what else would a million dollar drag queen use besides 100% pure mink brushes**? They are the softest brushes available, not to mention they last forever. I would rather pay for the finest brushes than have to replace them after every show.

Believe it or not, the tools you choose have just as much of an effect on the outcome of your face as the products themselves. **You could use top-of-the-line**

I highlight different parts of my face with blush to create different illusions.

cosmetics, but if the applicators are wrong, the outcome could be disastrous.

Now with all the outlines traced and all the colors in place, I sit back to admire my hard work with the same critical eye any true artist would use to examine his own masterpiece. I look for any noticeable flaws. I check my face from every angle. I smile and frown at my reflection. **I need to be one hundred and ten percent satisfied before I walk on stage.**

Even though I have spent the hour applying the perfect face, **I retouch my makeup throughout the entire evening so that it will hold up under the hot spotlights.**

Seeing as I have to go through this ritual almost every night, I have developed a great respect for the women in this world who have mastered the art of putting on makeup at red lights and stop signs. **Although, I'm sure very few of them are trying to cover up a five o'clock shadow.**

Now remember girls, the bigger the hair is, the smaller the hips look.

The final touch of the evening is putting on the wig. I have hundreds of different character wigs, but the ones I love most are the exotic up-dos. Which, thanks to my hairdresser, Gregory Andrews, is my trademark look. My hair always looks like a piece of art. People often ask how long it takes to style my hair. My standard answer is: **"I don't know. I've never been there!"**

One of the reasons my wigs always look so good is because as soon as they arrive, Gregory takes thinning sheers and removes at least 25% of the hair, which gives them a much more natural look, as well as making them easier to work with. Many women make the awful mistake of taking a new wig and placing it directly on their heads, right out of the box.

To me, nothing looks more ridiculous than a woman with more wig hair on her head than "Cousin It" has on his entire body.

Now if you think putting on the makeup sounds tough, just wait until you have to take it off! For the hour I spend designing the perfect face every night, I spend an hour-and-a-half taking it off! It's pure hell trying to get all that makeup off your face after you've had it on for six hours under hot lights. **The stuff is actually baked into your skin.**

Soap and water alone are not the solution. To this day, I've found that the only thing which works properly is Johnson & Johnson's baby oil. Despite old wives' tales that you will break out in pimples if you put it on your face, in fact it does quite the opposite.

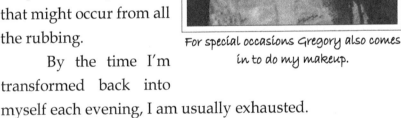

For special occasions Gregory also comes in to do my makeup.

It leaves my skin as smooth and soft as a newborn babies. Once I remove every trace of makeup from my face, I use a specially blended Scandinavian skin cream to prevent any rashes that might occur from all the rubbing.

By the time I'm transformed back into myself each evening, I am usually exhausted.

I often speculate as to why women would deliberately choose to do this to themselves on a daily basis, especially if they don't absolutely have to. I think every man should try wearing makeup at least one time in his life. I'll bet you dollars to doughnuts, they would never again rush their wives out of the bathroom. Nor would they expect her to be ready in fifteen minutes for a night on the town!

Remember:

Powder and Paint may give you the look, but baby, you gotta have the **Attitude** to do the rest!

My first head shot.

2

A Place to Call Home!

I was born November 20th, 1963, in Brooklyn, New York, a mere two days before President John F. Kennedy was shot and killed. I've noticed most people can remember exactly where they were or what they were doing the day the president was shot. My mother would sometimes joke about my birthday. She would often say: **"One great man came into this world, while one great man went out!"**

My mother and father holding me at my Christening the day J.F.K. was shot.

I was the only child of Sandra and Frank Marino, your typical Brooklyn, New York family. Because I was an only child, they spoiled me rotten. **I was never told no. If I wanted it, I got it!** I was showered with unconditional love and affection from both my parents.

My parents vacationing at Sea World.

Sadly, tragedy struck home when I turned six years old. I was destined to suffer the first and most devastating loss in my life. My mother had become ill with breast cancer. Within a period of several months after she was stricken, my mother was hospitalized, and during this same period of time my father was also diagnosed with lung cancer. Unfortunately, my father was too ill at that time to keep me with him.

Danny and Rosemary Marino.

At this crucial and frightening time in my life, **I was sent to live in Oceanside, Long Island** with my cousins, Danny and Rosemary Marino. Danny was the father of three sons, Danny Jr., Michael and Guy, as well as a daughter, Terry.

I'll never forget when I hugged my mother goodbye that afternoon. F**or some reason I just felt I would never see her again.**

The Marino Boys, Mike, Guy and Danny.

Now on top of the emotional devastation of being separated from my parents, I was forced to discover I was no longer

Me with Terry Marino. I'm practically pouting because I wanted the doll.

the center of attention. I would simply be looked on as one of the bunch. With four children of their own, there was little chance, if any, of being spoiled. Danny Marino was a sports enthusiast. His sons were always going to football or baseball practice after school. **My interests were always focused in much different areas. I enjoyed arts and crafts, board games and television.**

The last Christmas my parents ever got to spend together.

During the week between Christmas and New Year's, my father was released from the hospital for five days and came to take me home for the entire week. It was during that visit that he told me my mother had passed away just before Christmas. Since they were both very ill, they had promised each other that if one of them should die, the other would not tell me until after the holidays.

I was devastated and confused. I wanted my mother back. **How could it be she was gone forever?** I will never forget my father telling me that she went to live with the angels and that God needed her to live with him. I look back with hindsight now and realize that the devastation was so

My nephew, Damien, and my niece, Samantha.

severe at that age, that to associate it with Christmas probably would have created a whole new set of problems for me to deal with.

Dad took me back to Danny and Rosemary's house just after New Year's. I finished out the first grade with them. Here I was, a confused and lonely little boy, living with cousins who were totally convinced that all boys should enjoy rolling around in the dirt chasing after one shaped ball or another. **Not this boy!**

My godparents, Sarah and Ace Paz, who raised me as their son.

Four months passed and during Easter break my father worked up the strength to take me on a trip with him to Los Angeles, California to visit his sister, Sophie. **For a six-year-old kid you could imagine the thrill of seeing Disneyland for the first time.** This place made such an impression on me that to this day I still take my nephew, Damien, and my niece, Samantha, at least once a year to Disney World in Florida for a vacation, hoping that it will have the same happy effect on them as it had on me.

By the time summer came around, I had begun asking if I could go with my godparents, Sarah and Ace Paz,

My new family. Alan, Toni, Nadine, Sharon, John, Grandma, me, Grandpa.

who happened to be very close friends with my mother and father, and who also lived in Oceanside. They had four children of their own: three daughters, Sharon, Nadine and Toni, and a son, Alan. I always loved to visit them because they had the best toys. I especially loved when I got to play with their large collection of Barbie dolls.

The next year I got my wish and off I went to live with Sarah and Ace. I lived with them for the whole year that I was in the second grade and things seemed to be going great. That was until the following year when I started the third grade. I'll never forget when I came home from the first day of school; I found Sarah in tears. I immediately had that same strange feeling as when I hugged my mother good-bye that last time. I just knew in my heart that my father had died.

I insisted on going to my father's wake to see him for the last time. However, when we got to the funeral home, I just broke down in tears and could not bring myself to see my father in a wooden box. Therefore, Sarah and I just stayed in the car while Ace went inside. **To this day, I'll never forget seeing the six pallbearers carrying my father out to the hearse.** That was the most horrifying experience of my life. So, there I was, nine years old, both my parents had died within two years of each other and I was to live

Toni and I getting ready to carve the turkey.

permanently with my god-parents.

At this point, however, all my possessions including toys, pictures, and so forth were taken, grabbed and argued over by the rest of the family. **The house I called home had been stripped of all its contents.** If Sarah and Ace had not stepped in and warded off the vultures, I would have been left with absolutely nothing! The house was sold and liquidated, and was placed in a trust fund, which included a fistful of restrictions set up by my father in his will. One of which was that I graduate from college and that I could not touch any of the money until I was at least twenty-one years of age.

I was never legally adopted by Sarah and Ace, who, out of respect for my parents, believed I should keep the Marino name, although they raised me with the same love and affection they had for their own children.

Nadine and I making snowmen. I don't know who looks worse, us or the snowmen.

From my parents' deaths forward, the rest of my childhood was mostly a normal one.

In the beginning it was difficult to adjust – especially the first time Ace had to discipline me. I had never been spanked before. **I became very rebellious and insisted on having the last word. I would often prefer punishment to giving in!**

I think as I look back at that time in my life, I would have to say my parents' death and the loss of all my belongings by the family arguing over who was entitled to what, caused me to become a somewhat materialistic person. I vowed way back then that never would anyone take what was mine away from me again! I also learned that not everything lasts forever. **After all, everything I have now, could be gone tomorrow!**

Take this job and shovel it!

For the next four years, I started working very hard. I began with paper routes. There were times when I had two or three routes at the same time. It never mattered how hot or how cold it was, or how early or how late it got, I would just work, work, work. I raked leaves, mowed lawns, shovelled snow, and even took my sisters' left over baby-sitting jobs.

I did everything in my power to make money.

3

Macho, Macho, Man!

If you have ever raised a teenager, known a teenager or been a teenager, you know that at that point in their lives, they know everything! My teens weren't much different than anyone else's. I was making the B's and C's in school. I was planning my college career, hating the thought of four more years of school after the drudgery of high school, but **knowing that it was my parents' last wish, I would find the strength to suffer through it**!

Me holding my dog Tequila with my friend Peter Mazukiewitz.

Debbie Johnson and I in her home in Florida.

I did have lots of friends, like Peter Mazurkiewitcz and Debbie Johnson. I met Debbie in the first grade and remained friends throughout school. Her family was very wealthy and I loved her mother, Linda, **who reminded me of**

Debbie Miles and I at her sweet 16.

Crystal from Dynasty, with all her fancy clothes and jewelry. Another one of my good friends was Debbie Miles, a very tall and beautiful blonde girl. I also loved her sister, Pat, who was a model at the time. **I thought it was just the coolest thing to know someone on TV and in magazines.**

Looking back, I can honestly say I was always impressed with money. I seemed to be drawn like a magnet to the wealthier circle of people. **I liked all the beautiful things money could buy.**

By the time I was fifteen I began finding faults with myself that I was convinced needed correcting. I insisted I needed a nose job! Then again, back on Long Island wasn't everyone getting their nose done? If you didn't have a nose job, you were treading on thin ice socially. What would you possibly talk about at the next party you attended? I begged Sarah to let me have the surgery. It took some fast talking and teenage convincing, but eventually she gave in. So... at sixteen, I underwent the surgeon's knife for the first time and emerged with a brand new nose.

Debbie's sister Pat and I did a movie together called "The Long Run," about roller skating.

Along with my new nose came new interests. Suddenly, Disco music hit the air waves and I found a new passion in life! **Move over John Travolta; Frank Marino has learned to dance!** I do have to give credit where credit is due. John Travolta did introduce my wardrobe to white suits and black polyester shirts!

My Aunt Lucy, Cousin Joey, and Uncle Mike.

Disco was hot and there were hundreds of contests to enter and show off your talents in. Most of them were in Brooklyn on weekends which worked out great, because I could go and stay with my cousin, Joey, at my Aunt Lucy and Uncle Mike's house. One time when I was visiting them I met a girl named Laura Greco. Everyone knew that Brooklyn girls were so much more stylish than the Long Island girls.

Laura Greco was a Brooklyn girl who could Disco dance just as well as I did. **We entered a couple of contests together and won! The applause, the attention and the recognition that went with winning these dance contests were exactly what I was craving.**

I loved being the center of attention and had not felt the thrill of that luxury in several years. Once I was out on the dance floor, I was somebody. I was no longer just one of five kids. **I was Frank Marino, the Disco King!**

Little did I know that in several short years I would be Frank Marino, **the Las Vegas Queen!** But that's a whole different story and we'll get to that later.

Throughout the rest of high school, I would escape from Long Island into Brooklyn to Aunt Lucy's house almost every weekend, just to dance at the clubs. **I loved dancing, but even more so, I loved showing off.** Life was almost perfect. As perfect as it could be for a high school kid with a new nose and the ability to dance.

Laura and I practicing for the dance contest.

Somewhere during this magical era I turned seventeen, and a million different things happened that would later change the course of my life forever.

Shortly after I turned seventeen, I developed my first real case of **"Puppy Love!"** I developed a serious crush on one of my teachers. There were rumors going around school that this teacher was gay. I had never paid much attention to them until now. I don't think I can explain when or how it happened, all I know is one day I knew without a doubt that I was in lust with this teacher.

Having never felt this way before and not knowing what to do about it, I decided to write the teacher an anonymous letter telling him how I felt. Never in my wildest dreams did I envision the possibility that the teacher would recognize my handwriting. After all, this man graded papers for a living and probably knew each of his students' penmanship better than he knew their names. Well, lo and behold, that's exactly what happened.

I had my first crush on Mr. Loupi.
He became a great friend.

I didn't sign the letter but several days later the teacher asked me to stay after class for a minute so that we could discuss a paper I had written. **Right then and there I knew I'd been had!** Of course, he turned down my overtures. However, he did so with such compassion and understanding that my ego was only slightly bruised instead of severely crushed.

In the long run, that teacher did me a fantastic service. We had many in-depth discussions and he helped me learn to accept and to cope with my new found interests and sexuality. We had lunch several times after that, but strictly as student and teacher.

In retrospect, I now understand what I couldn't at that time. The man was doing his job. **He went above and beyond the call of duty to help me through what, at that time, could have been a major crisis in my emotional life!** Let's face it; do any of us ever forget our first crush? Though we remained student and teacher, we developed a friendship that we shared over the years. **Nothing sexual ever became of our relationship, but I valued his emotional support dearly.**

Me holding the roses I received after my performance in the Shakespearean play "A Midsummer Night's Dream."

Seventeen was also the age of proms and graduations! I was graduating from school and already enrolled in Nassau Community College for the fall semester. It was automatically assumed that I would attend my high school prom. So, at the age of seventeen, I asked my thirteen-year-old friend, Christine Rispoli from Brooklyn, to be my date for the prom. She was one of those more mature, stylish, Brooklyn girls I hung around with. We had a fantastic time at the prom. **We virtually shined on the dance floor as once again my dancing was the center of attention!**

My senior prom.

During this same era, there was a girl I grew up with who lived around the corner from me. Her name was Donna Pluma. She was a sweet person, but I was not interested.

Unfortunately, Donna fell in love with me. Sorry Donna, but now you know why

I couldn't return the feelings. I still have all your love letters tucked away in a shoe box in my closet! In fact, they are so well written, I would love to have them published.

Sorry, Donna, it would never have worked.

The next major event that I remember happening that same year involves my sister, Sharon, who was twenty-eight years old and married already. She and her husband invited me to go away with them for a weekend. I must have been blinded by the Disco lights. I had no idea that a whole other world was going on around me.

My high school graduation. (The first time I got to put on a gown.)

About two hours outside of New York City, on Long Island, was a resort area known as Fire Island. As far as I know, this was the only nude beach where sun worshipers could go without being disturbed, enjoy their devotion to both sun bathing and obtain the perfect all over tan.

While my sister and brother-in-law relaxed in the sun, I took a walk further on up the beach. Much to my surprise, there was another side of Fire Island that evidently was well known to everyone except me. There was an alternative lifestyle area, where gay males and lesbian women could worship the sun together without ridicule or harassment. There I saw open affection and concern between people of the same sex in public for the first time.

I'm not implying that anything sexual was occurring in public. What I am saying is that I saw men walking arm in arm with other men. The same applied to women. I am not claiming naiveté here, either. I just found it amazing as well as refreshing that here, at last, was a place where you could comfortably be whoever and whatever you wanted to be. **I had to get out in the sunlight more often! This night life was keeping me too much in the dark.** I started to go to Fire Island whenever I could make the time.

Even though Sharon was married by the time I went to live with the Paz family, we were still very close.

That same summer I managed to get a job to help pay some of the expenses I was bound to face starting college that fall. I secured a position as a junior pharmacist at Drug-A-Rama, a local pharmacy not far from my house. I worked mostly weekdays and evenings, which left my weekends free. **When I wasn't going off to Fire Island, I was dancing at the Discos in Brooklyn.** During my Disco dancing era, I developed an interest in other styles of music as well.

This is where I discovered the singer who became my idol and the most important role model in my life. It was then that I discovered Diana Ross!

As far as I was concerned, she had it all. She had both class and pizzazz. I began to lip sync to her music and emulate her movements in front of the mirror at night while I was getting ready to go out. Before the end of the summer, I could move almost as well as Diana could.

I was not aware of the significance this ability to mimic peoples' gestures would later play in my life.

4

Ghosts, Goblins, & Drag Queens?

Some time in October just before my eighteenth birthday, a close friend showed me a flyer from a night club called Starz. They were hosting a special Halloween night lip-sync contest and were offering a large cash prize to the winner. My friend suggested I enter the contest dressed as Diana Ross and do one of her numbers on stage.

I admit I was intrigued, but I was also hesitant. I had been perfecting my moves and lip-syncing for months, but I had never even considered trying to dress as her. Besides, how was I going to dance on stage in high heels? Hell! **How was I even going to walk on stage in high heels?**

I thought about it for several days. Finally, I decided to go ahead and enter the contest. The worst thing that could happen was I'd lose, right? I could actually think of a million things worse than losing, but what the heck. It was Halloween and what better time could there be to make a fool of yourself.

I still had my job at Drug-A-Rama, so one night with nothing else to do, I decided to check out the cosmetic department. If I were going to dress up as Diana Ross, I was going to need Revlon's help!

I spent days oohing and aahing over the different colors. **Before the end of the week it was obvious that I was spending more time in the makeup department in the front of the store than at the prescription counter in the back.** Preparation H, Visine, and Maalox could not compete with Cover Girl, Maybelline and Almay! I was hooked.

Even with my employee discount, I spent a large portion of my paychecks over the next several weeks on eye shadows, blushes, foundations, liners and please don't forget the lashes! At seventeen, my five o'clock shadow was already dark enough to resemble a total eclipse of the sun.

Buying this stuff was a breeze, since everyone at the store knew that my two sisters, Nadine and Toni, still lived at home. Hiding it from my family, well, that was a whole different story. **I would sneak my purchases into the house and squirrel them away to the attic.** There, among the forgotten toys and discarded valuables, I would spend hours in front of a full length mirror trying to perfect the art of applying makeup so that I'd look like Diana Ross.

I was so enthralled with this woman that I taped, tacked and stuck hundreds of pictures of her to the walls in my bedroom. I stared at them for hours on end, desperately trying to copy her look. In fact, there were so many pictures of Diana Ross in my room it looked like:

"A Harem in Harlem!"

Me and my friend, Susan, in my room getting ready for Halloween – the first time I was ever in drag. Notice all the Diana Ross photos on the wall.

When I was convinced I no longer looked like something out of a horror movie, I moved on to the next phase of self-inflicted torture.

The next step in preparation for the contest was to learn how to walk in high heel shoes. **I snuck into my sister's room and borrowed a pair of her "highest" heels.**

I spent hours walking back and forth across that attic floor. I would balance a book on my head in order to be able to stand up straight, look poised and not have my ankles collapse. Gradually, and painfully I might add, I eventually learned how to walk somewhat gracefully.

I looked as if I were dancing. By the time the contest came around on Halloween night, **I was hot! I was ready! I was... "Diana Ross."**

I walked on that stage with my head held high. Every hair, every fake nail and every sequin was in place. I lip-synced my favorite song of hers called "The Boss," which was a top Disco hit back then. I even pulled off a few dance steps in the high heels without breaking my neck. I felt the electricity in the air. The spotlights, the stage, the applause, I was ecstatic.

Me performing at Starz Halloween night as Diana Ross. This is where it all began.

I'm delighted to say all my efforts paid off that night. **I won "Best Costume"** and was approached by Greg Kramer of Universal Talent Showcase. He asked if I would be interested in repeating that night's performance at other clubs.

He left me standing backstage with his business card in my hand and my jaw hanging open. I was to call him the following week if I was interested. Interested? Yes, I was interested! Greg said he could set up some bookings in a few of the local clubs and see what kind of response I generated!

By the time my eighteenth birthday rolled around, I was in my first year of college. I was still working part time at Drug-A-Rama. I was still going to Fire Island on weekend afternoons; and now, I was about to add an even more complicated addition to my repertoire. I would be performing weekend nights dressed as Diana Ross! **I was going to lip-sync my way to fame and fortune!**

With all the sneaking around I was doing, I decided I needed a car. I could no longer depend on friends to get me where I had to be. I approached Sarah with the subject of buying a new car. She was adamant, "No new car." She felt the first car I owned should be a used one.

I knew I would have to take another approach. I went to my trustee, who happened to be a lawyer, and informed him I needed to have a car in order to continue attending college. I explained I could no longer depend on friends or public transportation. Between work and school, I was stranded without having my own car. I explained to him that if I got a used car and it broke down, I wouldn't have the money to fix it, so a new car would be much better in the long run.

The lawyer was very understanding and gave me an advance from my trust account. I took the money and purchased a 1981 Mustang.

Now that I had wheels of my own, I called Greg Kramer to tell him I would do any bookings he could get for me.

I was still sneaking to the attic to perfect and shorten the time it took to transform into Diana Ross. Even though I had two sisters living under the same roof, there was no possible way I could go to either of them for help. As a matter of fact, when it came to coordinating their outfits and

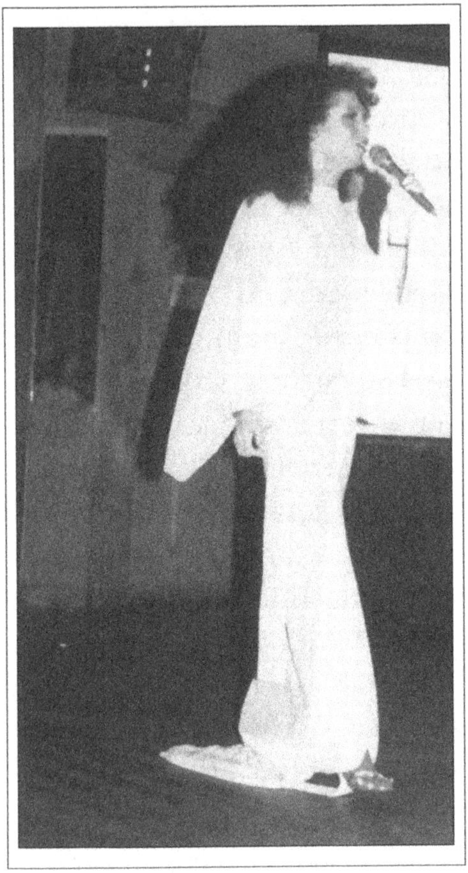

Performing as Diana Ross
at the Silver Lining Club
in New York.

color schemes, they often came to me for opinions and advice.

Greg was true to his word, he got me several bookings to appear at what I now know were seedy nightclubs. One of these gigs in particular stands out in my mind as something worth mentioning. I had been sneaking out of the house for several months now. I would always leave the house dressed in what I refer to as my boy clothes. **I would get into drag at whatever club I was performing in, usually in their filthy kitchens or basements along with the rats and roaches, and then I would change back again before going home.**

One night after a benefit show that I was doing with a dear friend of mine, Kenny Dash, who impersonates Joan Collins, I was so tired that I decided not to take the time to remove my makeup. My plan was to drive home in my bathrobe and shower when I got there.

It was late at night and I was sure Sarah and Ace would be fast asleep before I arrived. I jumped in my car and headed home down the parkway. I hadn't gone more than five miles when the car died. Damn, I thought the whole idea of buying a new car was to avoid this happening. I knew as much about cars and what made them work as your average insurance agent knows about performing brain surgery. **What a nightmare! Why the hell didn't anyone tell me you had to put oil in these stupid machines!**

Here I was in nothing but a robe, with a face full of makeup, stranded on the highway. I thought I'd take a chance trying to call home and hopefully one of my sisters would answer the phone. I could easily ask them to come get me and then have the car fixed in the morning.

I managed to get to a pay phone, drop in a quarter, and dial my home number, but to my surprise Sarah answered. She immediately asked where I was and said she would get Ace out of bed to come pick me up. I tried to weasel out of it, but Sarah wouldn't hear of me spending the night in the car. I had no choice. I had to tell Sarah where I was and hope she wouldn't put two and two together.

By the time Sarah and Ace pulled up to where my car was stranded, I had managed to wipe off some of my makeup. There was enough left, though, to know something wasn't quite right, but nobody asked any questions and I was not about to volunteer any answers. The three of us drove home in stone cold silence. There was never a discussion about the incident.

I'm extremely grateful for the fact that Sarah and Ace never seemed to pry too deeply into my personal life. They didn't question where I was going or why I didn't come home some nights until dawn. I guess they figured I was basically a good kid. They knew that I didn't drink or do drugs. As long as I was staying in school and working and staying out of real trouble, they probably thought they were ahead of the game. Although in those days, I often felt guilty as hell for having had to lie to them so often.

There was no way I could have ever told them the truth about my nighttime excursions. The fact that they had seen traces of stage makeup on my face that night only meant that I had been doing something unusual, not illegal!

DANCE CLUB & VIDEO CLUB
GRAND CENTRAL
Wednesday July 3rd
July 4th PARTY
2-4-1 Buffet
SATURDAY, JULY 6TH
Frank Marino as Joan Rivers
also appearing
Kenny Dash
The show I was doing the night my car broke down.

Things were cool and I could continue honing my skills in the attic for a while longer.

I knew sooner or later the truth would have to emerge. For the time being:

I was more than content
being a college student
by day and a
Female Impersonator
by night!

5

Finding Myself in Stitches!

During my second year of college, I discovered just how much I hated school. It was getting harder and harder for me to even fake being interested in what they were talking about. By the beginning of the third year, I had transferred out of Nassau Community College into NY University of Technology. I was bound and determined to finish my four years, only because that was my mother and father's last wish.

Performing as Diana Ross the night my sisters first came.

After many months of sneaking around, I finally confided in my sisters about my weekend activities. **In fact, I invited them to come see me perform.** I will say this much, whether they understood why I was doing female impersonations or not, they were very accepting and supportive of my choice. They took tons of pictures and congratulated me on my performance.

It wasn't until I started looking over the pictures they had taken that I realized **I looked like a big old man, in a dress.** A damn good effort, I might add, but not quite passable. My facial features were not soft enough to be feminine.

This is why it's so hard to get rid of that damn 5 o'clock shadow.

Being as critical as I was about the little details of my everyday life, it was a shock to uncover the fact that I had never noticed this during the hundreds of hours I had spent in front of the mirror perfecting my look. I forced myself to become more and more meticulous about how I applied the makeup in order to soften my male features. I kept striving for perfection. However, I was never quite able to get it feminine-looking enough.

So, once again I sought out and found a plastic surgeon to perform the surgery that I felt was necessary to refine the illusion I was striving to accomplish. Luckily I had managed to save some money from my performances, as surgery can be expensive.

Over the next two years, I went under the surgeon's knife again and again! I had a silicone implant put in my chin to fill it out and Mylar cheek implants inserted to lift my cheekbones.

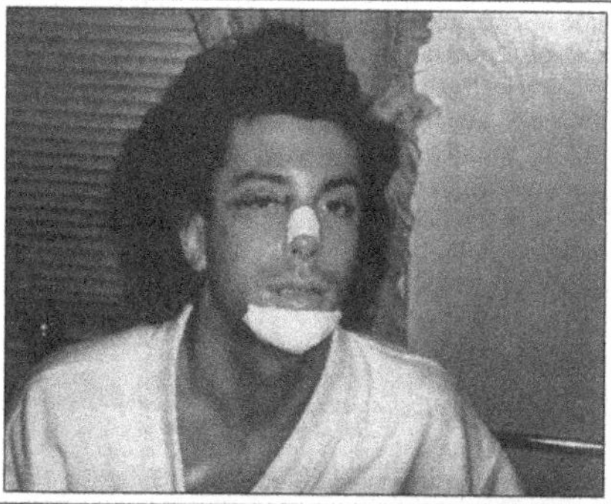

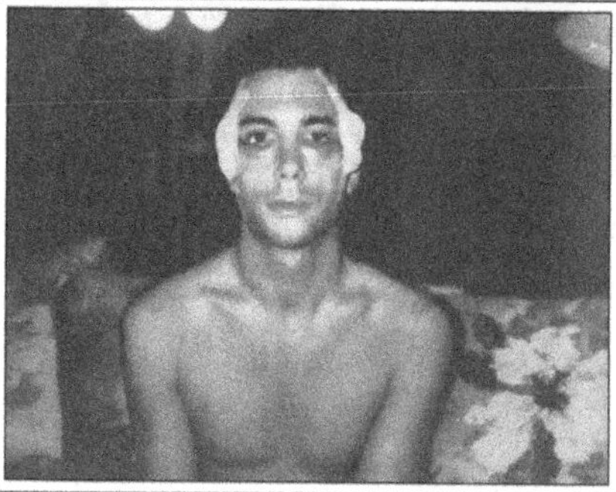

My motto was always,
No Pain, No Gain.

I had to take several weekends off in order to let the surgery heal properly. During the healing process I discovered I was no longer limited to impersonating Diana Ross. With my new high cheekbones, my softer chin line and my finely chiseled nose, I could be just about anyone I wanted to be.

My debut as Joan Rivers.

I began experimenting with different shades of makeup and hair.

I soon uncovered the fact that with a blond wig, and the right expressions, I was a dead ringer for comedienne Joan Rivers, who was one of the hottest and most popular female celebrities during this period of time. **Well, ok. Maybe a passable ringer if you'd already had a few scotch and sodas!**

I began focusing my attention in what little spare time I had to studying Joan's mannerisms on stage, and of course, her wardrobe. I spent hours upon hours playing and replaying tapes of Joan Rivers' shows. Then it was day after day in front of the mirror imitating her movements until I had them down.

The hardest thing I had to learn was her tone of voice, **because I wanted to perform this character live!** With Diana Ross, all I had to do was move my mouth and lip sync to a record. With Joan, well, that was something altogether different. I had to learn how to use comedy monologues and tell jokes. That required the power of speech. **I actually had to develop a talent for making people laugh at what I said!** Once again, not an easy task.

Performing in the discos meant getting ready in those horrible basements.

When I felt comfortable enough, I tried out my act on stage. To my surprise, I was a hit the very first time.

So, I started alternating my weekend appearances. I would lip-sync and dance my way across the stage one weekend as Diana Ross. The following weekend I would come out dressed as Joan Rivers and wow the audience with some jokes and monologues of what was going on in Joan's life at the time.

Also around this time, my hairdresser friend Rick came over to my house to give me a haircut; he brought the owner of his salon along with him; her name was Lucille

Out on the town with Lucille.

Bove. As it turned out, Lucille and I hit it off right away. We both like amusement parks and made a date to go to Great Adventure the following week. From there we started going out almost every day; she would even sit through classes at college with me if I promised to go to the mall shopping with her afterwards. We took trips to Florida, California and Las Vegas. I just loved it in Vegas and began dreaming of appearing on the Strip myself one day.

We went on all kinds of different adventures together and built a fabulous friendship.

Time seemed to fly by. Before long, I had put in my four years of college and was the proud holder of a Bachelor's Degree in Business.

My life was now my own! I had made my parents dream come true. That's when I finally broke the news to everyone:

I'm a Female Impersonator!
I'm going to be a
STAR!

6

The Truth Unfolds!

Around the time I turned nineteen **I started hearing rumors about my having been adopted.** There were stupid little things being said like: "I heard Frank is Jewish." With a name like Marino how could I be Jewish? This particular remark was said to Lucille by one of my cousins. As we were close friends, Lucille questioned me about the remark; but as many times as I questioned Sarah about why things like that were being said, she never once gave me a straight answer.

If Sarah and Ace had never adopted me, how could I have been adopted? I was bound and determined to sort this out once and for all.

Me, Sarah and my brother, Alan, at my cousin's wedding.

I finally sat Sarah down and braced myself for the confrontation that was about to take place. I knew if there was any truth to be heard, I was about to hear it. The question was, "Would I be able to deal with the truth? Was I really ready to know what everyone else already seemed to know?"

I looked Sarah straight in the eyes and asked her why I kept hearing that I was adopted! At first Sarah tried to avoid the question. There was the usual conversation about how much she loved me and how she had raised me as if I were truly her own son. I reached over and held Sarah's hand as I looked deeply into her eyes. I caught a brief glimpse of the pain and the sorrow she had kept hidden for so many years. I could see the desperate struggle she was facing. I also saw the resolve and conviction in her eyes as she came to peace with the fact that it was my right to know. It had been my decision to ask, and now **the time had come for the truth to be told**.

As the tears streamed down her face, Sarah told me the truth about my life. She said that my biological mother

Sarah with my sisters, Nadine, Sharon and Toni.

had gotten pregnant at a very young age. She was not married at the time, and there was no feasible way she could afford to keep me.

The Marinos, whom I thought of as my real mom and dad, had adopted me at birth. They had been unable to have children of their own and had jumped at the opportunity to adopt me. I had gone home from the hospital as Frank Marino, without my biological mother having ever seen me! Sarah and Ace were my godparents from the time I was christened. They had been best friends with my parents. When my mother and father took sick, Sarah and Ace raised me out of respect and tradition.

My entire life had been changed in a matter of minutes! I didn't know who I really was, until Sarah reminded me that: I was Frank Marino! I had never been anyone else. She assured me that even though my biological parents were out there somewhere, Sandra and Frank Marino were my parents. They were the ones who had loved me. Sandra was the woman who had changed my diapers and walked the floor with me when I cried at night. Sandra was my mother.

There were millions of questions I wanted to ask. Where was my real mother now? Did anyone know her name or how I could find her? What about my father? Did I have any sisters and brothers? The list went on and on.

In the meantime, sitting in front of me was the mom who had tolerated all my quirks and faults for the last thirteen or so years. **The mom who didn't have to love me, but chose to!** The mom who had taken over when my

Sarah and I were always close.

mother died! The most wonderful, caring woman I had ever known in my life.

I was almost twenty years old, and I had already survived the third most devastating period of my life. **I was beginning to wonder if my entire life would turn out to be one devastation and heartache after another**. I was wondering if I would ever be able to find happiness.

I felt as if nothing I had was ever really mine. I always had someone else's life, someone else's parents, and someone else's identity. **No wonder I'm a female impersonator!** I even pretended to have someone else's

Who is Frank Marino?

gender! Now it was my turn. I wanted to have something that I didn't have to share with anyone else, ever again.

Each time I began to feel sorry for myself, or if I dwell on my sorrows and disappointments too long, Sarah's words come back to comfort me. I can still hear her saying,

"You can do anything you want to do.
You can be anything you want to be.

You just have to be
willing to work hard
at it and you can
make it happen!"

7

Leaving the Big Apple for Some Florida Oranges!

Two months after I started impersonating Joan Rivers, I had gone to see her perform on stage in Atlantic City. Surprisingly, I was invited backstage after the performance and even managed to have my picture taken with her. It was this photo which I later used in my ads. I thought people would be impressed with it and give me the better bookings.

The first time I met Joan Rivers, Atlantic City 1982.

Sick thing, but it actually worked! That same night, Joan Rivers introduced me to Lou Paciocco the producer of

La Cage (a world renowned female impersonation revue).

I was thrilled to discover that Joan was impressed with my impersonation of her. From that moment on, I could feel the bond of friendship building between us. Thanks to Joan, **Lou offered me the opportunity to fly out to California to his club in Beverly Hills and audition for the starring role of his new La Cage Show in Florida as Joan Rivers.** I was thrilled at the offer being presented to me. This would be the first real recognition I had received for all my efforts.

Although, there were a multitude of problems I had to face regarding the offer. It would obviously mean moving to Florida; that is, of course, if I got the job. Then I would have to tell my manager, Greg, that I'd be leaving him. Of course, there was also my job at Drug-A-Rama and my new boyfriend, Robbie, who worked as the manager of a Hallmark-type of store called Goodies, located next door to Lucille's hair salon. As a matter of fact, Lucille was the one who introduced us to each other.

Robbie just hanging around the house.

Robbie was about six feet tall with blond hair and blue eyes. Lucille told me she thought Robbie and I would hit it off as well as she and I had. Lucille was right. **From the time Robbie and I met, there was a certain electricity**

in the air! I wasn't sure, however, if I would be able to convince Robbie to move to Florida with me.

I made the trip to California with notable anticipation. I wanted this part more than anything else in the world. **I just knew that my entire future revolved around getting this job.** I aced the audition and was offered the starring role in the show.

I returned to Long Island after that audition knowing full well that I would be moving to Florida as soon as I could pack my belongings. All that was left for me to do now was explain my decision to leave home.

Over the next few weeks, I spent all the savings I managed to accumulate while working at Drug-A-Rama and doing my weekend shows, on custom made evening gowns. **I knew before I arrived in Florida, I would need a minimum of 20 outfits in order to be able to change the required number of times per show.**

Give my regards to Old Broadway.

The day finally arrived when I had to say good-bye. I packed up my makeup, shoes and, of course, my wigs.

Now at last, I had paid my dues and earned the opportunity to pursue my dreams. When I left that day, I said my tearful

Landing in Florida with only $535.00 in my wallet.

goodbyes to Sarah and the rest of my family. As I loaded up the cab, I looked back and there on Sarah's face was a glow and a smile, along with a tear in her eye. As I turned and got in the cab, Sarah shouted out, "We love you!"

I knew right then and there that from that point on, everything else would be ok. **I was now alone and on my own.** All too soon, I was on the plane headed for Florida and my new life.

I had been rescued from the low rent district of entertainment. I was on my way to Florida and being given my first opportunity at stardom. Not to mention all the free orange juice I could drink.

I quickly realized the difference between doing the show in those seedy little nightclubs and actually performing on a real stage. I was committed to one show per night, six nights a week. When I was doing nightclub shows, I could get by with one, sometimes two, gowns per night. Now, I had to change fifteen times per show. Each and every night. I only had the twenty or so gowns so my choices where limited. **Help! I need more gowns!**

My opening night at the Sunrise Musical Theater in Florida.

It was at this point I called upon every seamstress in town to make me more and more costumes for the show. This was the beginning of my clothing addiction.

As I think back to my first few days in Florida, I recall a time that was not all wine and roses. **When I arrived in Florida, I had a total of five hundred and thirty-five dollars in my pocket,** since I had spent the rest of my savings on the gowns.

Alone again, naturally. Just me and my twenty gowns.

I arrived at the airport; obviously I had no car; therefore, I had to rent one. Since I didn't have a credit card at that time, not to mention any credit, I had to put up a five hundred dollar deposit. That left me with thirty-five dollars to my name. Lou Paciocco and his brother, Anthony, who would later become my new manager, **put me**

Me with Lou Paciocco's brother, Anthony, and his girlfriend, Debbie. Anthony later became my manager.

up in a beautiful penthouse and paid my rent. At least I didn't have the worry of having to find an apartment. That night after my first show, they took me and the cast out to dinner. The following night after work, they invited us all out to dinner again.

By now I had already spent the remaining thirty-five dollars on groceries, which left me broke until payday. This time Lou tried his hand at some dry humor.

Just as we were getting ready to leave for the show and head out for dinner, Lou looks over and says, "By the way, Frank, it's your turn to pay for dinner tonight." **I wanted to die! I was flat broke.** I had to pretend my wallet was stolen in order to avoid being totally embarrassed.

My two best friends in the whole wide world Fluffy and Maxine.

Little did I know ten years later I would be able to buy that same restaurant, in cash!

By the time I had fully unpacked and settled

Whoever said money can't buy happiness
doesn't know where to shop!

in, I was getting very lonely being away from all my friends and family. I didn't want to come home to an empty apartment anymore. I couldn't wait for Robbie to come and join me. In the meantime, **I went out and bought myself two puppies, a girl Schnauzer, Maxine; and a boy Lhasa Apso, Fluffy.**

Aside from the unrequited crush I had on my teacher, Robbie had been the only other serious "relationship" in my life to date.

So, other than being alone, everything seemed to be going my way. **My salary had jumped from a hundred and fifty dollars a night, two nights a week, to more than fifteen hundred dollars a week.**

I had a beautiful penthouse and I was thoroughly convinced life couldn't get much better than this. I really thought I had it all, and I was only twenty years old.

Now that all the little details had been worked out and I was all settled in, it was time to call Robbie and have him join me. The day he arrived, I was overwhelmed to see him standing there.

As the weeks went on, I realized **I was falling in "LOVE."** It wasn't a puppy love, nor a high school kiddy crush type love. It was more a special, true and actual, forever type of love. Robbie and I spent every available moment together. He even took a job as a stagehand with La Cage. This allowed us to be together even more often, plus it altered our schedules so that we were both working the same hours.

It's lonely at the top but the view is spectacular.

Robbie was the perfect complement to my personality. Yet still, I was never satisfied with what I had. I always wanted more. I had this desire to be perfect, and I strived to be the best at everything I did. I loved my job, but I still felt the need for more in my life. I guess I would have to say I lived by the old adage, **"Once you think you're done, you're dead!"** At twenty, I was far from being ready to just lie down.

Robbie never tried to stifle my creativity. In fact, he was always there encouraging me. He would often remind me of the fact, that **"Everyone loves a winner!"**

It was because of Robbie's constant praise and encouragement that I continued to advance my career. **I still had my dream of one day seeing my name in the marquee lights on the Strip in Las Vegas.** I knew the only way to make my dream a reality was to work even harder. I threw myself into my work with every ounce of energy I possessed.

Looking back, I guess that was part of what came between Robbie and me in the long run. Even though he was a hundred and fifty percent supportive of my dreams and desires, **I always put my career ahead of our relationship.** I was always under the impression that he would be there when I got where I wanted to be. I never suspected I would lose a part of myself and Robbie along the way.

I pushed myself to the limits. I began seeking all the attention I could get. If the press was around, I was there.

There is one time in particular during this era that stands out like a sore thumb in my mind. I had received a call from the Miami Herald asking if they could send a reporter the next day to interview me. I was thrilled.

That morning I went downstairs to see the doorperson. I explained that there would be a reporter coming out to interview me and I needed to make a good impression. I solicited her help in making me appear slightly more, shall we say, in demand than I was at that point. I handed her a stack of handwritten messages. Of course, they were all fake. I then asked that when she called to announce that the reporter had arrived, could she call me Mr. Marino instead of Frank? To add fuel to the fire, I also asked that she give the stack of messages to the reporter for me since she was on her up anyway.

Some of the most beautiful women in the world are men.

I knew full well that if this was any type of reporter, she would read the messages on her way up in the elevator! They were messages from MGM saying they needed to speak with me; Bob Mackie saying my gowns were ready; so on and so forth.

The next morning I set my alarm clock for seven, knowing the reporter would be there by eight. I got out of bed, threw on my sweats, spread my weights out all over the living room floor and waited for the buzzer to announce the reporter's arrival.

When my buzzer rang at precisely eight, I sprayed myself down with water to make it look like I was sweating. When I answered the door I faked being out of breath. Since my penthouse overlooked the golf course, I made a point of telling the reporter I had just gotten back from my morning jog. Between the weights strewn across the floor and the soaking wet sweat shirt, she bought the story hook, line and sinker. She was very impressed with the amount of time I spent working out.

Little did that reporter know, if it were not for the interview she was doing that day, I wouldn't have gotten up that early for anything! Even if I had to pee, I would prefer to keep a bedpan next to my bed.

Needless to say, the story she did turned out terrific. It made me sound absolutely fabulous. **From there on in, I couldn't be stopped!**

If there was a contest to be entered, I entered it! If there was an extra appearance to be made on my night off, I made it. **I was the definite workaholic.**

I had one goal and one focus in life. Nothing was going to get in my way or slow me down. There was nothing or no one who could stop me from becoming:

"The Best
Female Impersonator"
the world had ever seen!

8

A Broad in the Riviera!

I was working in Florida and everything was going along great when the owner of the Riviera Hotel in Las Vegas, Meshulam Riklis, who was married to Pia Zadora at the time, made a reservation to see our show. **I thought to myself that this could be the big break I was waiting for.**

He was very impressed with the show and decided it would be perfect for his hotel. He went back to Las Vegas and built an entire wing onto the Riviera and called it the Mardi Gras Plaza. They were going to add three new showrooms and La Cage was going to be the biggest of the three shows. They designed a room called the La Cage Showroom which was

Gambling with my future.

very avant-garde: black walls with zebra-striped rugs. It was as modern as modern could be.

I had a two-month break while this was all being put together and had moved back to New York with Robbie and my dogs for the entire summer.

I finally convinced Robbie to move to Las Vegas with me. I promised him it would be great.

It may have taken me years, but I was finally on my way to Las Vegas. I wasn't sure I could make it there, but I was willing to give it one hell of a shot! This is where I had dreamed of performing my entire career. As Robbie and I stepped off the plane, I felt as if I had truly made it.

People go to Las Vegas to get rich! So did I, but I also wanted to be famous!

Once again I arrived at the airport without a car. This time, renting the car was much easier. I now had a credit card. Funny what a year in Florida can do for you.

Thanks to my new manager, Anthony Paciocco, my salary had once again jumped, this time from **$1,500 a week to more than a quarter of a million dollars a year**. I was on my way to the big time.

When we arrived at the hotel the sight that greeted me made the entire struggle to get there worthwhile. There on the side of the hotel was a life-sized marquee which read:

"An Evening at La Cage, Starring Frank Marino as Joan Rivers."

The first time my name was on a Vegas marquee.

My dream had come true. I had worked and slaved and played some of the seediest nightclubs in the Tri-state area. I had dressed in kitchens and basements with rats and roaches running up and down the walls. I had snuck out of my parents' home, hidden my clothes and makeup in the attic. I had gone home from work hungry and had to fake having lost my wallet in order to not be embarrassed in a

The La Cage Billboard.

My dream come true!

restaurant with my producer. **I had, without a doubt, paid my dues and served my absolute apprenticeship.**

Florida was fun and I enjoyed the time I spent there but, honey, this was my new home. This is where I had wanted to be my entire life! **This was a dream come true!** A dream I still don't want to wake up from. I was not going to let anyone or anything get in my way. **I would make this town sit up and take notice of me.**

I had long ago discovered that dressing up in women's clothes was not enough to make it in this business.

Opening night in Las Vegas.

Yes, drag pays well! However, you had a much better shot of being taken seriously if you were able to perform as a celebrity look-a-like. I knew I did a fabulous Joan Rivers. However, fabulous was never good enough for me. **I wanted to be the best there ever was.**

I began pushing myself harder and harder. I spent hundreds of hours perfecting my act. It didn't matter that I had been doing Joan for several years already. Being good and being the best were two totally different things. Besides, I had a new goal in mind now. It wasn't enough that the billboards said: "Starring Frank Marino," I wanted my name to be as important as the show itself.

My producer, Lou Paciocco, my new manager, Anthony Paciocco, and my new producer, Norbert Aleman, had set me up in a fantastic condominium. It was lavishly furnished and bigger than most houses. I was being wined and dined. For the first time I actually began to feel like a star!

The only man I've ever met who had more glitz than I did.

As soon as I was settled in, **I called Sarah and invited her out to Las Vegas** for my opening night. I'll never forget that night. It was magical.

I met Liberace, who later introduced me to Anna Nateece, who made all his fur costumes. I remember him saying he thought she would be perfect for me.

Liberace's designer, Anna Nateece, making me my first fur coat, which almost endangered an entire species.

Sarah had long ago accepted the fact that I had to wear women's clothing for work. As a matter of fact, she actually enjoyed the advantages my dressing as a woman afforded

Sarah at my show
in Las Vegas.

her. Let's face it, **how many mothers could borrow a dress from their son?**

Sarah had become extremely supportive and proud of the road I had chosen to take. She was beginning to see that what I was doing each night was a profession and a career, not just a whim, or a fantasy to dress up in women's clothes!

She was so comfortable with what I was doing that she actually laughed when I incorporated this little joke into my show:

I think my Father would kick my ass if he ever saw me in this dress… It's HIS!!!!!!!

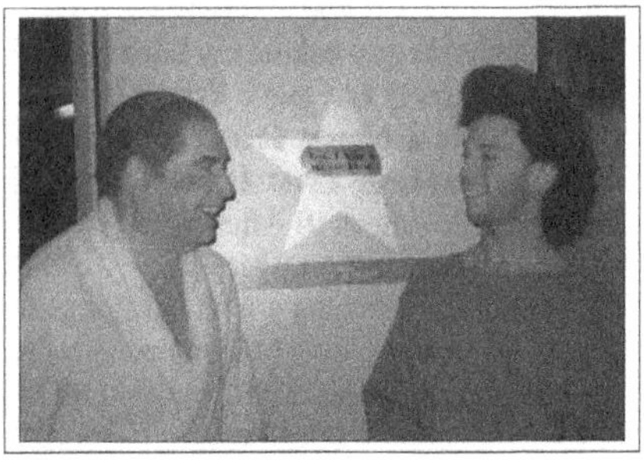

Getting advice from the father of television, Uncle Milty.

Not long after I arrived in Las Vegas, I had the opportunity to appear in a television special called, "Milton Berle Joins La Cage."

He was to be the host and I was going to be one of the acts. The idea was that we'd battle back and forth on stage. He would tell a fat joke, then I'd tell a fat joke. He would tell an ugly joke, then I'll tell an ugly joke. Before the end of the night we were laughing as hard as the audience was.

I had invited Robbie to watch the filming of the special. It was during the taping that Robbie ended up

Poverty Sucks!

All work and no play is what made me the fabulous Drag Queen I am today.

sitting next to the boyfriend of one of my dancers. One week later, I overheard Robbie on the phone making plans to meet with this guy behind my back. I saw red!

I was not going to pay for that "Don Juan" to live in my house while he was out painting the town. I asked him to move out. I couldn't believe it! After three years together, he was making plans to cheat on me.

I felt as if the rug was being pulled out from under me. This was the person I thought I wanted to spend the rest of my life with. Robbie decided to spend the next few months living with my two cleaning ladies, Sandy Schone and Georgia Roscow, a mother and daughter team that worked for me on a daily basis. But eventually Robbie decided it would be better to move back to New York. It took me years to overcome the pain of losing Robbie. To this day I still have a special place in my heart for him. So once again, there I was all alone and on my own.

Around this same time Joan Rivers proved to be hotter than ever. She was in all the national magazines and on every major TV network. **Not to mention the fact that she was the permanent guest host on "The Tonight Show" when Johnny Carson was off.** Joan was one tough female comedienne, which is what I idolized most about her. **I never wanted to be a femme-fatale. I have a strong personality and I wanted to emulate a female star with the same characteristics.**

Now with Robbie gone, I had a lot of extra time on my hands and work was the only thing that brought me any joy, so it was back to the tapes and the mirror to perfect my impersonation of Joan Rivers. It was also back to the plastic surgeon.

All totaled, I ended up having nine surgeries. My cheek bones probably have more silicone in them than Dolly Parton's TITS! Not to mention all the chin, nose and jaw work I've had done! I had long ago learned to regard the surgeries as my ultimate sacrifice to fame. It was the very least I could do in order to achieve the perfection I demanded of myself! If all it took were a few cuts, some stitches and a few black-and-blues to achieve my goals, then by all means, Doc, stitch me up!

By the time the surgeons finished nipping and tucking my face, I was a dead ringer for Joan Rivers. I looked more like Joan Rivers than Joan did! Let me add that it wasn't easy for a twenty-one-year-old man to look like a

Two of Hollywood's biggest bitches.

fifty-two-year-old woman. I even began having my clothes made to match hers. I even used a few of her lines in my act for realism's sake.

I enjoy my job and that's what it has always been, "A job." I have never had an identity crisis.

I have never wanted to be "Joan Rivers." I have met many impersonators who lose track of who they are. They

Strike a pose.
Me as Madonna.

Not such a sure Bette.

start living and breathing their character to the extent of losing touch with their own identities. They actually become "Elvis, Marilyn Monroe or even Madonna." The biggest thrill I get out of doing what I do is that I get to see life from both sides, male and female. But who the hell wants to walk around in a push-up bra, high heels and pantyhose twenty-four hours a day if they don't have to. Besides, I've impersonated so many people, unless I was "Sybil" it would be impossible for my characters' personalities to take over. I've tried everyone from Madonna to Bette Midler.

I'll never forget the first time I decided to do Bette Midler. I was in a major department store, (let's just say the first initials were JC_ _ _ _ _,) there was a mannequin that had the exact same red, curly hair that Bette Midler had. I'm embarrassed to say this, but I snatched that mannequin bald so she looked like Sinéad O'Connor, and that night I too looked like Bette Midler. **Since that time, I have spent so much money in that store I'm sure I've repaid them over and over again for the little gift they gave me.**

While I was in Las Vegas, Joan Rivers and I were becoming better friends than ever. I spent lots of time with her on different occasions and had even been invited to her house for dinner. She took the time to introduce me to the designer who made several of her gowns and had even given me some of her old comedy material to use in my act. **I cherished the friendship that Joan and I developed because it gave me the opportunity to get to know the woman I impersonated firsthand.** I discovered that she had exactly the same strong personality both on and off the

Eat your heart out, Carmen Miranda. Me with good friend, Larry Alarid.

stage. For that, I admired her even more. She truly seemed supportive and proud of my talent to imitate her.

My career was in full swing. I was headlining one of the hottest shows in Vegas. What more could I ask for?

I can't even begin to mention all the stars who came to see the show, just to see who was impersonating them that week! Their usual response was laughter, a hug and congratulations on getting their personalities and movements down so precisely! I never had a star stop me after the show and tell me either I or one of the cast had insulted them.

I guess the old saying is true:

"Imitation
is the Sincerest
Form of Flattery."

9

Will the Defendant Please Rise...

The summer of 1986 was a time of many trials and tribulations for me. The pain and sorrow I experienced are etched deeply within my heart.

The down side of that summer was the fact that Joan Rivers, a friend of mine and one of the people I idolized most, turned against me. I had already undergone the surgeon's knife repeatedly. **I had spent in excess of fifty thousand dollars having more parts of my face lifted than an abandoned Mercedes**, just to look like the object of my admiration! I would have done anything to please her and have Joan smile down on my humble efforts. I knew she understood my respect for her, since I had always portrayed her in the most flattering light, and up to that point in my career we had a terrific rapport.

The drama began early one evening while I was on stage performing to an audience of close to a thousand people, looking like a young porcelain version of Joan Rivers. As the music from "The Tonight Show" played in the background, I was handed a subpoena which stated that

Joan Rivers had filed suit against me. I was shocked, astounded and hurt.

Instantly, the lawsuit made headlines. The press flocked to the story like pigeons in the park. Suddenly, I was the object of a media blitz. They examined and inspected every detail of my life. I was flooded with more publicity than I ever could have afforded, or generated, on my own. It was apparent that this lawsuit would serve to make a series of firsts.

For the first time ever, an impersonator was being sued by the actual celebrity.

UNITED STATES DISTRICT COURT
DISTRICT OF NEVADA

JOAN RIVERS,

Plaintiff,

-against-

FRANK MARINO, NORBERT A. ALEMAN, LOUIS PACCIOCCO, and HOTEL RIVIERA, INC., d/b/a HOTEL RIVIERA,

Defendants.

STIPULATION OF SETTLEMENT AND CONSENT ORDER

CV-S-86-769 RDF

WHEREAS, the defendants have the highest regard for Joan Rivers ("Rivers") and her reputation as an outstanding performer and comedienne;

WHEREAS, the impersonations of Rivers referred to herein were intended and performed as a reflection of her celebrity status and her enormous impact upon the public, and were further intended and performed as a respectful satirical and/or comedic interpretation; and

WHEREAS, the uses of Rivers' comedy material alleged in plaintiff's Complaint, to be Rivers' material, all of which is denied by defendants, were intended to enhance said impersonations;

WHEREAS, Rivers instituted this action on August 11, 1986 after various requests were made by Rivers, in an amicable manner, to the Producers of "An Evening at La Cage" (the "Production") and to the impersonator of Rivers in the Production, to eliminate Rivers' comedy material

The legal papers between Joan and myself.

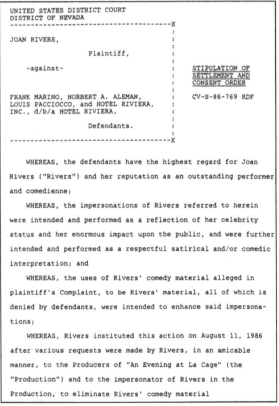

NATIONAL 65¢
ENQUIRER
LARGEST CIRCULATION OF ANY PAPER IN AMERICA
STAR'S FATHER A PAID KILLER
s' Bartender Tormented by Tragic Family Secret
Joan Rivers Threatening To Sue This Female Impersonator — He's Using My Jokes
Wedding Fever
Mike Wallace's Wacky Wedding: Maid of Honor Was A Man — And Best Man Was a Woman
James Brolin 'Weds' While Not Legally Divorced — Exclusive Interview
Prince Andrew: At 158 Lbs., Fergie's Not Too Fat for Me
Caroline Kennedy To Henpecked Groom: Your Total Involvement in This Wedding Is Just to Show Up at Church

I was featured on the front cover of the National Enquirer, making tabloid history!

The lawsuit had a price tag of five million dollars attached, which literally knocked my feet out from under me. As I paced the floor backstage reading and rereading all the legal documents, my mind drifted back to happier times. I just couldn't believe she would do this to me. This had to be some sort of joke.

Or was it? I smiled as I thought of the times I had spent telling interviewers how Joan had given me the name of her dress designer and how we had decided that between us we were keeping the plastic surgeons in business. I immediately relived the feelings I experienced the time Joan announced on national television: **"He's having surgery to look like me. I'm having surgery not to look like me. I think I'm going to end up looking like him!"**

For the next six months, the attention the "battle" with Joan Rivers received catapulted me into the limelight. Besides being on the cover of the National Enquirer, which appeared in hundreds of thousands of check-out lines and magazine racks from coast to coast, I also made appearances on TV shows like "P.M. Magazine" and "Good Morning America." Even USA Today and Playboy magazine did stories on me.

My public recognition level skyrocketed tremendously, not to mention the sellout crowds at La Cage. However, the relentless stress was taking its toll on my relationship with my producers as well as my own peace of mind. Until now, I had been emceeing the show as Joan Rivers. I viewed this position not as a job but as a dream come true! I was just developing my stage routine, so I didn't have many comedy skills yet.

Now, according to the lawsuit she filed, I was being accused of lifting her jokes and "stealing" her comedy. All of this came about after my local competitor (who shall remain nameless) went to Joan's people and said that I was doing her exact routine. **(Well, I was impersonating Joan Rivers. Whose act should I do, Roseanne Barr's?)** I guess she didn't like my stand-up routine being so close to her own line of patter on stage.

Jealousy among the competition in the field of female impersonation is something I have learned to deal with on a regular basis. However, I was not prepared for one of my competitors to drive a wedge between myself and

Joan Rivers, especially since we had shared so many tender moments together as friends.

The lawsuit Joan had filed had named my producers and the Riviera Hotel, as well as myself, which only added to the enormous pressure I was under. There were millions of dollars in liability at stake! Tension was mounting and tempers were hotter than the hundred and sixteen degree Las Vegas summer heat.

ITS THE MOST TALKED ABOUT SHOW IN AMERICA–YOU'VE SEEN IT ON THE COVER OF THE NATIONAL ENQUIRER, ON P.M. MAGAZINE GOOD MORNING AMERICA AND ENTERTAINMENT TONIGHT
ENQUIRER
STAR'S FATHER A PAID KILLER
Lou Paciocco & Norbert Aleman present
AN EVENING AT
La Cage
Starring FRANK MARINO
as a carbon copy of Joan Rivers

I have to admit, I felt such conflicting emotions, fear of failure and doubt of my own abilities to continue. Underneath it all, there was a gnawing sensation that a turning point was about to be reached in my career. Was I ready to go for it?

From where I stood, there was only one way out of this lawsuit. **I was facing a sink-or-swim situation.** After all, I was a celebrity impersonator, not a comedian yet! But I had to become one, quick. It was a hard lesson to learn, and there

Dragging myself to the bank to get that five million dollars.

was no time to learn it. **I had to become a true stand-up comic and find the talent I needed within myself!**

Despite great advice from one of my mentors, Milton Berle, who, when I was in the middle of filming the TV special with him told me: **"If you ever come across something funny… Steal it, kid!"**

I was beginning to learn firsthand there is a fine line you just don't cross! The time had come for me to develop my own routine, without using any of Joan's material, be it old or new.

Luckily, after six months of sheer and absolute torture, we were able to reach an amicable settlement in the five million dollar lawsuit. For that, I am extremely grateful, since at the time **I was about eighty dollars short!** A settlement was reached out of court whereby I could continue performing as Joan, provided I didn't use any of her material! I wasn't even allowed to say,

"Can We Talk?"

Can we talk? I couldn't say it so I displayed it!

Eventually, the dust settled and the show did go on. I'll never forget my first show featuring my all new, original material. I started to hear the audience cheer as I swept out onto the stage in a three thousand dollar Versace gown and a black foxtail boa wrapped around my arm. Please, Please, Please! For all you animal lovers out there: **I didn't kill it! It just died... and left me everything.**

The ends justified the means.

The audience was standing and roaring with support. I stood there gazing out at that wonderful group of people so full of encouragement and support, with my mouth dry and my eyes wet. I was overcome with respect and gratitude for each and every one of them. I knew something then that I had never really understood before. **I belonged to this world of entertainment! I was going to be okay after all!**

I would never recommend to anyone that facing a financially devastating, possibly career-crushing lawsuit is the way to go about becoming famous. Although I must admit, Joan Rivers may have dealt me a less than perfect hand when she slapped me with that lawsuit, but the press and all of the public interest generated by the lawsuit put me in the limelight and I am very grateful to that "Impersonator" for causing such a scandal, because thanks somewhat to his actions I became the number one female impersonator in the world.

"I now know
I'm where I belong!
And I'm here to stay!"

10

A Hair-Raising Experience!

I have had literally thousands of men and women come up to me after each performance and ask where they can get their hair and makeup done to look as good as mine. Finally, after answering this same question for years, I decided to try my hand at being a business mogul. In addition to my La Cage show six nights a week, **I decided to open my own full service hair salon where** I'd have a staff of professionals to create a multitude of different looks for both myself as well as for the people of Las Vegas.

When I decided to do this, I had no idea what owning a business would be like. That was, until I was in too deep to back out!

I look like a gay rooster.

I equipped the salon with everything anyone would need to perform haircuts, hair colors, manicures, pedicures, facials, tanning, and make-overs.

Of course I named the salon:

Frank Marino's La Cage.

Would you expect anything different? My motto read:

"You Too Can Be A Star.

Or Just Look Like One!"

With all the advertising I did, along with all the press I was getting, the salon attracted a lot of local celebrities! However, most of my customers were people who lived in town. You know the type. The typical upper middle class men and women who wanted a bit more glamour in their lives. Those who could afford the high price of luxury and enjoyed being pampered and catered to. The first customer I ever had was Joyce Rich, a waitress from the Riviera hotel. **When we had finished Joyce's hair and makeup, she looked like a supermodel.**

Move over Priscilla,
I'm Queen of the Desert.

Blondes don't always have more fun.

Sometimes too much is just enough.

Polly want a cracker?

If this isn't a throwback to the Seventies, I don't know what is.

José Eber was a great help to me when I first opened my salon.

When I first opened the salon, I copied a few little tricks from the ritzy salons in Beverly Hills, like Jose Eber's Salon (who, by the way, gave me many tips on how to run the place). I picked up the little things that make a person feel special. For example, I would have a fruit and cheese table set up, which always included sparkling water and a delicate fruit punch. We would use real crystal glasses and china cups and plates, not plastic! One of my personal favorites was, after doing a perm on the customer's hair, instead of rinsing

Feathers can always make a look.

it with plain tap water, **I instructed my hairdressers to rinse with Perrier**. The bubbles acted like an astringent against the scalp, causing a tingling sensation that signified clean.

Looking like
Breathless Mahoney.

Many of my customers would often comment on another little touch I always thought worked well. Instead of mixing their hair color in a tub or a plastic bottle, **I recommended my staff mix the colors in oversized crystal champagne glasses.** I knew that it was a lot of extra work for my hairdressers, but hell, I felt if they wanted to keep getting the big tips they were getting, they should be willing to work for them.

By George, I think I've got it.

I have been told on several occasions that I am a bear to work for and I guess I can understand why. I employed twenty hair-dressers, most of them were girls. Still, I couldn't understand the day to day problems they had. They would call in with an excuse like **"I can't work today. My pinky hurts and I can't hold the scissors."**

"Is it my imagination or am I starting to look like Barney?"

I tried time and time again to explain to them I also held a full time job and there was absolutely no way I could call in for every little ache and pain or inconvenience that occurred in my life.

I was always being accused of not being sympathetic or compassionate. I would tell my hairdressers if they were truly sick, then by all means call and let me know. However, I would not consider a broken fingernail a life-threatening illness.

My secretary, Loretta Mann, kept my books in order while I kept the salon in order.

Playing makeup artist at my salon.

I will tell you this much. **Being the star of a show did not prepare me for owning my own business!** I had no problem with all the paperwork, ordering the supplies, and customers' complaints and everything else that comes with the territory. I just couldn't deal with the whining of my staff.

I remember this one incident in particular which, to this day, still brings a smile to my face. I had hired one manicurist in particular, who was very flamboyant. After being on the job for about a week or so, she began showing up for work looking like a cross between Madonna and a cheap hooker. I tried once, then twice, to be polite. I asked her quietly if she could tone her dress down just a little. She'd say: "OK! no problem." Then the very next day she'd show up in something even tackier.

Test shot for Vanity Fair Magazine.

Finally, one day everything came to a head. **She showed up for work in a skimpy, lacy top and a skirt so short, she could have been a crack dealer!**

I couldn't take it anymore. I walked up to her and not so politely informed her that this was a hair salon and she needed to show up for work well groomed and much more conservative. She suddenly spun around, glared right into my eyes and announced: "If I had your money to spend on clothes, I would look as good as you do."

As the curtain of red clouded my vision, I retorted: **"Actually, I was thinking more along the lines of a little soap and water!"**

As for my clients, most of them were absolute dolls. However, I remember one lady in particular who came in

When you've got it, you've got it.

with a wig. She informed me that she wanted to look like Eva Gabor; in the meantime she had a neck like Edith Bunker! I almost told her it was impossible, but stopped myself just in time.

Bingo!

Getting ready to shoot a TV commercial for the salon.

Then of course, there were the women who would come in and say, "I want something I can just wash and shake that would look good." My standard answer to that request was, "If you're going to spend fifteen minutes on your hair, you're going to look like it! If you spend thirty minutes on your hair, you'll look like that. So it's up to you. You can either look like hell or you can look good. The choice is yours."

Finally, I decided to hire a manager for the salon and things began to run much easier.

Then on my twenty-fifth birthday, the staff threw me a surprise party. My life actually seemed to be running smoothly again. The day of the party, I walked into my salon and immediately made eye contact with someone across the room. **There were instant fireworks!** It was the new hairdresser my salon manager had hired. Now, here I was staring at one of the most gorgeous people I had ever seen. You know the type, six foot, black hair, blue eyes.

Suddenly, I found myself fascinated by a total stranger. As I walked over to introduce myself, I could feel my heart pounding in my chest. I was in lust!

On my 25th birthday all my friends dressed up as Joan Rivers look-alikes.

Several hours later, I was in love. I fell hard and I knew I was heading for trouble. Unfortunately, once again it was a one-sided situation. There were too many obstructions in the way for anything more than a fantastic friendship to develop. **It took me five years to realize I could never build this into a relationship.** I tried. I wined and dined. I teased and I tempted! For which I got no emotion in return. To this day we have one of the most honest, sincere friendships anyone could ever ask for.

Me with my best friend, Russ, who later bought my salon. Thank God!

With all the crazy shit that was going on in my life, I finally decided it was time to sell the salon and find something less time-consuming and less stressful to get engrossed in. I ended up selling the salon to a dear friend of mine,

Russ Bono. He has since moved the salon to a new location and renamed it "Russ Bono and Company." One good thing did manage to evolve from the middle of all that mess.

I produced my own line of Frank Marino shampoos and cosmetics which I still get orders for to this day!

11

God Save the Queen!

The year 1989 had to be one of the worst years of my life.

For some reason all hell broke loose! I was preparing to go on stage one night when my producer, Norbert, and I got into a big argument. At that particular time I had a dressing room with a view of the Las Vegas Strip. As the argument escalated, I stormed into my dressing room, slamming the door behind me. I yelled through the locked door, "I quit." Talk about a temperamental bitch! Norbert was pounding on my dressing room door demanding that I let him in. I was screaming back: **There's no problem. There's no need for a discussion. I QUIT!**

Norbert and myself at the five year La Cage Anniversary.

He kept banging on the door, yelling at me to let him in. I threw myself down on the couch, picked up the phone and proceeded to call my

Barbie and Ken – me and my good friend, Jahna.

friend Jahna to let her know that I was furious and had just quit my job.

Sometime during the course of my conversation, it became eerily quiet on the other side of the door. I wondered briefly what was going on. However, I really didn't care enough to get up and go find out!

I was laying on the couch pitching a bitch about how badly I thought I was being treated, when suddenly through the open window behind the couch Norbert appeared. I screamed! He jumped! Luckily, he fell in the window and not out. Especially since we were on the fourth floor of the hotel.

He had gone through the cast's dressing room next door. He then climbed out on the ledge, and while hanging on to the building, he shimmied across the little catwalk and climbed into my window. When he came into the window he was as white as a ghost, and as red as the devil, both at the same time. Thankfully, though, he had managed to keep his balance even when I screamed. I have to admire his determination. This was my first clue that this man gets what he wants, one way or another.

It's no secret that Norbert has always been extremely hard on me. If my salon employees thought I was tough to work for, they should try working for him. He usually criticizes almost everything I do. **He has forced me to grow up and see life as it really is.**

Nobody gets in his way, and nobody gets a free ride! He is a very strong-willed person who insists on having things his way. Norbert has taught me not to take any crap from anyone. He once told me that when you are the best, the world will step aside for you. I would constantly ask him if I could go to different functions, TV shows, or celebrity events. He would always say no; it's his favorite word. The man speaks seven different languages but knows the word no in twelve.

Once again in retrospect, I think he believed that if I got too big, I'd leave La Cage and go out on my own. **When is he going to wake up and realize that if he just lets me grow, I would have no problem staying forever?** I don't want to go out on my own. I'm content to remain where I am.

One of the other conflicting incidents I had with my producer was when I recently spent $40,000 on my new opening number. I had a large marble staircase built with huge roman columns and two colossal six-foot-high brass chandeliers. Along with all this, I had six tuxedos with crystal rhinestone buttons designed for my dancers, along with top hats, cummerbunds and bow ties. I also had Stephen Yearick, "A Famous Fashion Designer," and my good friend, Daniel Storey, create the outfits I'd be wearing. **It looked like the ballroom scene from Beauty and the Beast. It was Fabulous!**

It took me over six months of hard labor to complete. I personally designed the whole set to fit in the allotted stage area that I was given to work with. I also had to make sure

Performing my new opening number.
I'm one of the girls who's one of the boys.

the set would fit in the storage area when it wasn't being used on stage.

The chandeliers had to be big enough to be seen from the audience yet small enough to be flown in on a track. There is also a quick change that I do in the middle of the number behind a dressing room screen. I had to make sure the screen could be brought on in one piece, then break into two pieces so that I could come through the middle of it in the new outfit.

I handpicked every piece of fabric for both the set and the costumes so that everything matched perfectly. I also spent days making sure every note of the song I was going to be performing was perfect.

We did a trial run for Norbert, and would you believe all he could say was, "I don't like the way you move your hand." All the money, time and effort I put into this project and all he noticed was my hand. I don't think we will ever see eye to eye.

Speaking of eyes, another battle we're constantly having is Norbert thinks I should wear the little bi-focal glasses that Joan Rivers wears to read while I'm on stage performing. I refuse to wear reading glasses on stage with a beautiful evening gown, although this past year when we signed the new contract, we finally came to a mutual agreement. We compromised.

Glasses and glamour do not mix.

After I do my showgirl opening number, I promised that when I first come on stage as Joan Rivers, I would wear the glasses for the first few minutes to give the audience the initial look. Norbert thinks I look older with the glasses and that's better for the illusion. I don't think anybody, including Joan Rivers, would wear reading glasses while wearing a beaded gown. Even if they needed them, they would probably wear contact lenses. Anyway, the compromise was that I would wear the glasses and he would let me wear all the crazy hairstyles I want through the show. **Maybe miracles do happen!**

One of the people at work whom I love is Norbert's wife, Marlene. She is one of the nicest women you would

Marlene and I at a Barry Manilow concert.

every want to meet. She was a dancer prior to her marriage to Norbert, and now she often has the tedious chore of being a go-between and a mediator for Norbert and myself. **She has often been my saving grace and was one of the main reasons that I re-signed my present contract.**

I also consider myself a somewhat dominant personality. Nevertheless, I know when I have to be submissive! **I know that I have to lose some of the battles if I want to win the war!**

These incidents with my producer were the spark that ignited the forest fire which would continue to flare up uncontrollably throughout my fourth year in Las Vegas.

The second incident followed shortly thereafter! I loved the condominium that my producer rented for me. Nevertheless, I wanted a house. I wanted a home of my own. I decided to have one built with everything I wanted, where I wanted it and in the colors I wanted it in! Everything was going along smoothly. The contractors were pretty much on schedule.

They had finished off the inside and had very little to do on the outside to bring this project to total completion. In fact, they were working on the dog run when the second disaster struck.

Recording my first song with my friend Karen, the star of Splash.

No, it wasn't a flood, an earthquake, or any other natural disaster. I should be so fortunate. Those would have been more convenient and so much easier to deal with.

I had just finished furnishing the inside of the house. Everything was gorgeous! It had taken me months to hand pick each and every piece of furniture. Each picture, each statue, carefully inspected and hand chosen to match the décor. A totally different motif in each room, I might add.

It was close to Christmas and I had invited my entire family to my new home for the holidays.

I had the Christmas tree set up in the formal living room and all the presents beautifully wrapped under it. **Everything was in place and looked gorgeous!** I was extremely proud of all the choices I had made. I was sure

My new home in Las Vegas.

Sarah would be impressed with my selections. Hence, I was anxiously awaiting their arrival so I could show off all that I had accomplished.

Since the contractors were still working on the dog run, I was isolating my two little dogs, Maxine and Fluffy, between the laundry room for warmth and the garage for going potty. The first thing I did every night when I got home was clean up after the dogs. That's one of the reasons I was pushing the contractors to finish up. Anyway, I was coming home from work one night just weeks after moving in. As I turned the corner, I noticed the light in the cathedral ceiling skylight of the master bath was on. I was surprised. Usually I was very careful and meticulous about things. I remember thinking, **"This isn't Motel 6, and I didn't leave those lights on!"**

Watch out Caesars Palace, Frank Marino's pool is finished.

When I turned the second corner and headed for the driveway, I noticed the garage door was wide open. My heart skipped a beat! My first thought was that the dogs had gotten out. I was petrified. Where would they have gone? Would I ever get them back? They were like my kids! They had been with me since Florida.

I convinced myself to calm down. I knew if the dogs were gone, they were gone. Running in there helter skelter throwing the door open, wasn't going to change anything. It would not have accomplished anything more than walking in calmly would have. I parked the car in the driveway and entered the house through the front door.

To my surprise and utter delight, I was greeted at the door by both my little dogs. My first reaction was: I bet the cleaning lady locked them in the house by mistake. Now I'm going to have to hunt down and clean up the mess.

I never even noticed that my house was a total wreck. I had been so upset over the possibility of the dogs being gone, I didn't even notice there was mud all over the tile floor and muddy footprints all across the white carpeting. Not to mention there was no furniture, no presents under the tree. Nothing! **The house looked abandoned.**

As I walked into my bedroom, the first sight I saw was the wall where the TV used to be! Not only was there a hole, but the drywall had been ripped completely off the studs. My closet doors were open, allowing me an unobstructed view of a completely empty closet. They had taken everything. My boy clothes, whatever girl clothes I had at the house, my shoes, jackets, jewelry, you name it, they had taken it.

As I explored the house further I began to notice the obvious. Everything was gone! All my carefully chosen possessions had been stolen. I walked into the kitchen and that's when I noticed the French doors leading out to the patio banging back and forth. Just outside the doors, lying there in the mud, was my new bedroom television set.

I rushed over to the kitchen counter where I kept my phone. There I discovered, not only had they ransacked my house, they had taken the time to make lunch for themselves. Half eaten sandwiches and empty soda cans were all over the place.

I have never felt so violated in my life!

That was when it hit me. What if I had walked in on them? They might still be on the property. I immediately dialed 911. The realization that they could jump out at me from behind or come back through the open door scared the hell out of me. I scooped up my dogs and went to sit in my car in the driveway to wait for the police to arrive.

When they finally got there, I filled out the necessary paperwork, answered all their questions and was politely informed not to hold out too much hope of getting any of my things back. How nice.

That night, I plugged in the television that had been lying in the mud outside. Amazingly, it still worked. I fell asleep with it on, only because the noise was comforting. Besides, I was still worried that whoever had broken in would come back. My thoughts were if they heard the television playing they would realize someone was home and just leave. The following morning I awoke to the news playing on the television. All of a sudden I heard,

"Local Celebrity Impersonator Frank Marino gets robbed."

When I went out to the driveway and picked up the newspaper, I was in for an even bigger shock. Not only was the story of the robbery on the front page of the newspaper, the paper gave such a detailed description of the event that the story did everything but give people directions to my house. I mean, why not? Let them all come rob me again. I felt like hanging a sign on my front door saying, "Don't bother to break in, guys. The door's open. Help yourself!"

Is it any wonder that since that terrifying, eye

Doing a photo shoot for People magazine outside my home in Las Vegas.

opening incident, I now have bars, gates and an alarm system on every door, window and access point in that house? **The very next day I went out and purchased a hand gun**. I took a course in gun safety and several shooting lessons just in case! I wanted to make sure, if I'm ever home when someone breaks in, **I'll be able to shoot. Shoot, yes. Hit? Well, maybe. But I sure as hell will try!**

By the time Sarah and my family arrived for Christmas, I had replaced a large portion of what had been stolen. I was not quite as proud of my house as I had hoped to have been. I didn't have as much time or energy to devote to decorating the second time around.

I had barely recovered from the shock of the burglary when a close friend of mine was impersonating Madonna at one of my favorite nightclubs. I had promised to lend him a costume for that particular show. I went to the club and parked my car in a well-lit area. I was not inside the club for five minutes. Not five minutes. I swear.

When I came out, my car was smashed to pieces. Every window was broken! Every door was smashed in. I was taking some of my furs to Anna Nateece (the furrier Liberace turned me on to) so she could store them for the summer. I had them lying on the back seat of my car. In the blink of an eye, they were gone. Along with them went my car phone, all my paperwork (which was strange for me, but my secretary Loretta had been taken ill and was in the hospital, so I was doing the books myself), my money, as well as everything else in the car was gone!

I had my custom license plate which read "La Cage" on the car, so whoever did this knew whom they were doing it to. **Once again, I had to call the police, maybe I should have kept them on speed dial!** This was becoming a regular habit.

Since that wonderful little experience, I have developed a fear of parking my car anywhere with anything in it. If I have to leave the car anywhere for any length of time I lock everything, regardless of its value, in the trunk. One good thing emerged from that incident. Since I frequent that club so often, they gave me my own parking space.

I'll also never forget one particular night six months before I sold my hair salon; I got a call saying the shopping center was on fire. I jumped in the car and flew right over there. As it turned out, I was the only lucky one in the entire center. Every other store had been extremely damaged.

They had recently built a new fire department a few blocks away so that when the call came in, they were able to arrive in just a few minutes. That was the only reason they were able to save my salon. The worst I experienced was a lot of smoke damage. **I think, if it had burned down, I probably would have been living in Club Med by now with the insurance money!** Then again, as usual, life goes on. I managed to get it all cleaned up and reopened better than ever.

To add insult to injury, as if I had not been through enough in those last few months! That same year I had to hire a new cleaning lady to take care of my home because Sandy and Georgie had decided to move to California. While I was at work one evening, the new girl threw either a paper towel or a makeup tissue (at least that's what I think it was), in the commode which clogged the pipes. She must have done it as she was leaving for the day. I don't believe she would have left had she known what was happening.

When I came home that night, what I knew as my living room was now an Olympic-size pool! Apparently, whatever she tried to flush stopped up the toilet and it had been overflowing for the last eleven hours. When I walked through the door that night, my dogs were swimming around the house, and I found myself standing:

**Knee high in shit,
just like my life had
been that year!**

12

Reunions with Mom and Joan!

One night after my show in Las Vegas I met this amazing woman. She told me that she was in town for an adoption convention and did searches to reunite families and loved ones who had been separated for whatever reason. I, of course, asked her millions of questions and then asked if she thought she would be able to help me in locating my birth mother. She said it would be no problem at all, and would be more than happy to help me.

It wasn't but two weeks later that **I received a call that the search was over and they had found my birth mother.** Her name was Mary Minucci. I think I went into shock. After years of wondering who, why and where, I was now in possession of the phone number of the woman who could answer so many of my questions. Although at this point, I wasn't sure if I was really ready to meet her face to face.

I waited about two years until one day when my friend, Carol, from Florida was visiting, and somehow we got on the subject of adoption. I told her I'd found my birth mother but never contacted her. Carol felt that I should, if for no other reason than to find out medical history.

The next day, that's what I did. I decided to call the number I'd been given. It took a moment after she answered the phone for me to actually speak. **I asked her if the day November 20, 1963, meant anything to her, because that was how the search agency advised me to go about it.**

Mary was ecstatic and knew I was her son. She said she would love to meet me. She then explained that she was married and had a family. Mary admitted that she always wondered about me, where I was and if I was okay. She told me she had only been seventeen years old when I was born and that she couldn't afford to raise me on her own. Therefore, she felt that by allowing me to be adopted I would have a much better chance at a good life. She answered all my questions and insisted that the next time I was in New York we get together.

It wasn't long after that phone call, I had one of the biggest highlights of my career. **I was invited to appear on the Joan Rivers show. Talk about being thrilled!** Not only would I finally be working alongside the lady I impersonated after years of animosity between us because of the lawsuit, but I have to fly to New

Arriving at the Joan Rivers Show.

Performing on The Late Show with Joan Rivers.

York to do the show and this would give the opportunity to meet my birth mother.

The show topic was called, **"Joan for a Day."** There were three boys and one girl all dressed up as Joan look-alikes.

Here we were, two years after the lawsuit, sharing the same stage. I was standing there in a black and gold Bob Mackie gown. Yes, I was finally able to afford one. I know, I know! **I have dropped so many names in this, I bet you're getting a backache trying to pick them up!**

Joan was so gracious. She put me up at the Plaza Hotel, gave me my own private dressing room, while the other four guests had to share a much smaller one. She also provided me with a limousine for the day. She couldn't have been any nicer or more accommodating to my needs. She even asked me:

"Hey Frank, did I sue you? Or did you sue me?"

Keeping up with the Joans.

I really can't find enough words to say how exciting it was for me to be able to rebuild my friendship with her. She was the springboard to my career and to be invited on her show was an absolute dream come true. After the lawsuit, I would never have guessed she would have been so warm and friendly to me ever again. **That day Joan treated me more like a best friend than a guest on her show.**

Since I had the limo for the entire day, I figured I'd have the driver take me to meet my birth mother. When we arrived at the address, I was surprised to find that the stretch limo was nearly as long as the entire city block. Of course, when this **huge limo** pulled up in front of her house, every neighbor came out to see what was going on. I guess it looked to them as if Mary had won the sweepstakes and this was Ed McMahon coming to hand her a check for ten million dollars. **I stepped out of the limo and stood there looking into the eyes of the woman who had given birth to me.**

Of course, there were tears, hugs and introductions all around. I met her husband, Lou, my half-brother, Louis, his son, Louis Jr., and my half-sister, Nikki. It was a lot to digest in the short time we had to share. Eventually, we took our reunion inside. During the rest of our visit, Mary

My half-brother, Louis, my birth mother, me and my half-sister, Nikki

answered each and every one of my many questions. I asked her about my biological father and she informed me that the entire episode was a bad experience and I would be better off not finding him.

The first time I met my birth mother.

Looking back to that first visit, I find it amazing how certain things just seemed to fall into place. Mary seemed to know without my saying anything that I was in show business. **Maybe it was the stretch limo or my outrageous clothes.** When I told her what I actually did for a living, she was not really surprised. Somehow, it just didn't seem important at the

Knowing how to make an entrance.

time. There were so many stories to tell and such a short time to tell them in.

I can't really say I had felt any maternal feelings that day, but I felt as if I had made several new friends. Mary wants everyone to know I am her son and even though her new husband is not my father, he is very supportive of the whole situation. I actually feel as if they were an extension of my own family.

At this point I didn't want to hurt Sarah, so I never told her I had found my birth mother. I had convinced myself that she would be upset, or think that I didn't appreciate everything that she'd done for me. Words alone cannot define the gratitude, love and respect that I have for her. When I decided to tell my life story, I felt that it was important to include this chapter in the book because so many adopted children who've had awful experiences or suffered even more rejection when they find their biological families. As for me, I consider myself very fortunate to have had a good experience with my birth mother and her new family, so I felt it was necessary to tell the story.

Since there are only seventeen years between Mary and myself, we are more like good friends than mother and son.

To all the other adopted kids out there, I would just like to say that I consider myself lucky.

Being adopted means being chosen!

I have had three sets of parents, where some people only have one. Six sets of grandparents where others have two. I have several half-brothers and sisters and an entire army of aunts, uncles and cousins.

I have often been asked how I feel about having been adopted. If there is resentment or hatred toward my birth mother because she gave me up. All I can say **is I don't look at it as her giving me up. I like to think she gave me a chance. She gave me an opportunity to have the type of life she couldn't give me.**

I definitely thank her for being strong enough to do what was best for both of us.

I knew before this book hit the stands I would have to face Sarah and tell her the truth. I dreaded the hurt I knew I might cause her. But, I also knew there was no other way. I was very nervous about having to tell her the truth. I called her and began to ask how she'd feel if I tried to locate my birth mother. She was very supportive. In fact, she actually asked if I wanted her help.

Since she took it so well, I explained that I had already located and had the opportunity to meet my birth mother in person. There was a dead silence on the other end of the phone which seemed to extend for all eternity. Finally, I asked Sarah if she was OK. Sarah asked how long ago I had found her. When I explained that I met Mary and her family about three years ago, Sarah quietly whispered: **"Frank, your birth mother's name was not Mary!"**

Sarah went on to explain that she knew people who knew my birth mother and that she was personal friends with the doctor who delivered me. I felt as if the wind had

Since my parents' deaths, I've always considered Sarah to be my mother.

been knocked out of me. I could barely follow the rest of the conversation. Sarah was sure my real mother's name was Corine, not Mary.

There had to be some mistake. **How many seventeen year old females with the last name Minucci could have given birth to baby boys on 11/20/63 and given them up for adoption?** I had been assured that the woman I had contacted was positively my mother. We looked exactly alike. Now I was being told none of it was true.

I spent the next few days frantically trying to locate any and all the information I could from the Bureau of Vital Statistics in New York. My temper was flaring and my nerves were stretched to the limit. At one point, it was recommended I have a DNA test to satisfy my curiosity.

Decisions, decisions, decisions.

Now the problem I faced was whether I should pursue this further or should I simply accept the fact that the odds were actually in my favor that Mary was my mother.

After all, the paperwork made sense and everything seemed to add up correctly. But that nagging little voice inside my head kept saying, "If she's not, then you still don't know who you are or where you came from." **The only conceivable thought I could come up with was to have the DNA test and find out the truth, once and for all.**

My sister, Nadine, who works for a blood bank, gave me all the information on how to begin the procedure.

I was soon to discover you couldn't just set up an appointment for a DNA test. You needed an attorney or a doctor to order the testing. I called my doctor in Las Vegas and he set up the appointment for myself and Mary. She would have the test done in New York while I would have mine done in Las Vegas.

We were taking a test called the Buccal Swab test. This type of test involves obtaining a DNA sample by scraping the back of the throat. This test is said to be 99.75% accurate.

In the meantime, I decided to go back through my family history and called Danny Marino. That's the first person with whom I lived after Sandra and Frank Marino became ill. Danny also knew people who supposedly knew my birth mother in the same manner as Sarah did. Danny also thought the girl's name was Corine and that the father's name was Louis.

The only thing that made my story stand very strong was that Danny Marino gave me the adoption papers and the last name on those papers was Minucci, which was also Mary's maiden name when she gave birth at the age of seventeen. Now for Corine to be my mother, it would mean that her last name would also have had to be Minucci. But the chances of two young girls with the same last name having a baby on the same day and giving them both up for adoption was very unlikely.

Through this entire ordeal, Sarah kept insisting that both of my biological parents were only fifteen years old, so it couldn't be Mary because her boyfriend was much older. The stories just did not match.

Sarah had hundreds of arguments. She knew the girl. She knew the doctor. She even knew the boyfriend. This whole thing was starting to make me crazy.

Sarah also said that my biological mother had begun looking for me fifteen years ago. She was ill and wanted to meet her son before she died, but my family kept her away.

At one point Sarah decided to look up Mary's number in the phone book. She called her and asked her several vital questions that she thought she knew the answers to. Questions like, "How old was the father? What hospital did you have the baby in?" Mary answered the questions by saying that the baby's father was much older than she and that she didn't remember the name of the hospital. It was so traumatic **she had deliberately blocked it from her mind**. Sarah couldn't understand how somebody could forget where they had given birth. Sarah knew for a fact that the mother had become pregnant by a boy who was only fifteen at the time, not older.

After about a week of stories going back and forth, Danny Marino tracked down Corine's mother through family friends. To my surprise, Corine did, in fact, exist. Although the twist to the story was simple; Corine's last name did not match the last name on my adoption papers, which was Minucci. **Corine's last name was listed as Fiorri.**

With this twist, I thought maybe the babies had been switched in the hospital. It wasn't until I called Corine's mother to get more information that I found out Corine did not have her baby boy until December 6th, 1963, which meant **I could not have been that baby, simply because I had already been Christened two weeks earlier, the day John F. Kennedy was shot.**

So with this new information, I was one hundred percent sure that Mary was my mother and what had happened was the doctor had given Mary's baby to the

Marinos and Corine's baby to another family. If there was any misconstrued information, it was through the fault of the doctor.

Four weeks after Mary and I went for the DNA tests, the results came back.

The results are in!

LabCorp
Laboratory Corporation of America
P O Box 2230 Burlington, NC 27216-2230

Page 1 of 1

Account Information
Acct # [illegible]
JERRY CADE MD
Acct Ref 1
Acct Ref 2
Acct Ref 3
LAS VEGAS, NV [illegible]

LabCorp Case # C96-042399

Relationship	Party		Race	Date Drawn
Mother	MASTROANGELO, MARY L	675-2305-0	Caucasian	[illegible]
Child	MARINO, FRANK V	673-2326-0		[illegible]

DNA Analysis

	D1S80 1,2 (1p36-p35)	CSFR 1,2 (5q33.5-q34)	FES 1,2 (15q26.1)	VWF 1,2 (12p13.3-p13.2)	FGA 1,2 (4q28)	CYP19 1,2 (15q21)
M	25, 29	7	3, 5	6	3, 4	6
C	18, 29	7	3	4, 6	3, 5	3, 6
PI	5.04	1.77	1.56	2.63	0.75	1.37

DNA Analysis

	ACTBP2 1,2 (6q)	TH A,B (11p15.5)
M	4, 25	7, 10
C	20, 25	10
PI	7.89	1.35

Conclusion:

The alleged mother, MARY L. MASTROANGELO, cannot be excluded as the biological mother of the child, FRANK V. MARINO, since they share genetic markers. Using the above systems, the probability of maternity is 99.75%, as compared to an untested, unrelated woman of the North American Caucasian population.

Combined Parentage Index 400 to 1

Probability of Maternity 99.75%
(Prior Probability = 0.5)

Lloyd C. Osborne, Ph.D

Sworn to and Subscribed before me this JUL 1 7 1996 at Burlington, N C

"OFFICIAL SEAL"
Notary Public, North Carolina
County of Alamance
Josephine Foust
My Commission Expires 10/24/98

Laboratory Corporation of America is accredited by the American Association of Blood Banks, the American Society for Histocompatibility and Immunogenetics, and the College of American Pathologists

Mary was indeed my mother.

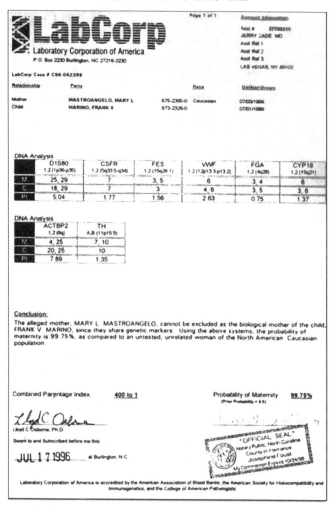

To this day nobody knows what the mix-up was. Corine did, in fact, have a baby boy, but that baby was not given to the Marinos. If, in fact, the Marinos were told that the baby they were getting was Corine's, or if they just assumed that the baby they were getting was hers, is something that we will never know.

I'm glad to find that Mary is my mom. I'm also happy to say I've since heard that Corine did find her son fifteen years ago before she passed away from leukemia. Her son's name is Philip and he resides in New Jersey.

I don't know how things got so confused, but I'm glad that we can now both enjoy the relationship we have developed over the years without any shadow of a doubt hanging over our heads.

Mistakes Do Happen,
But This one was made
out of LOVE!

13

Talk Show Junkie!

From the time the Joan Rivers' show was aired, my phone began ringing off the hook. I was now receiving calls almost on a daily basis to appear on other talk shows all over the country.

By now, Joan and I had come full circle. We had been friends, enemies, and now, we had a blossoming friendship once again. I had long ago realized she actually did me a favor when she filed that lawsuit. Inadvertently, she had thrust me into the limelight of the press.

Filming the "Gossop, Gossip, Gossip" commercials for Joan Rivers.

Now that we had become friends again, Joan couldn't be more helpful with my career. At one point she actually took time out of her busy schedule to film a segment of **"Entertainment Tonight"** with me. And then she gave me the great honor of asking me to do eight promo spots for her talk show, **"Gossip, Gossip, Gossip."**

When I had finished filming these commercials, it started to become more and more difficult to allocate my time for all the shows that wanted me to appear as a guest, due to my already overwhelming schedule. I had to pick the ones I thought would do the most good and turn down the rest.

I turned down **"The Jerry Springer Show."** I watched a few of his episodes and in "my own opinion," he had no talent as a talk show host. He seemed to be scraping the bottom of the barrel. He never offered his guests any help. He seemed to get a kick out of exploiting them. I felt he was just interested in the sensationalism.

On the Vicki Show.

One of the talk shows I did decide to accept was the **"Vicki Lawrence Show."** The topic of the show was: **"Can you guess who's the male, and who's the female impersonator?"**

The show was scheduled to have a male and female Cher, Whitney Houston and Madonna impersonator, then there would be a female Joan and myself as the male Joan Rivers impersonator.

After Vicki talked to each of us, the audience would decide which the female was and which the male impersonator was. The audience guessed correctly on the Chers and the Madonna's. However, when it came to myself and Didi Hanson, who was the female Joan that day, **the audience guessed wrong!**

Vicki couldn't believe the response when Didi and I revealed our true identities! I was shocked to be chosen as more realistic than an actual female.

I later appeared on the **"Montel Williams Show."** Montel, by the way, just happened to be married to a friend of mine, Bambi Jr. Bambi used to be one of the stars of "Crazy Girls," which is another revue produced by Norbert and also plays at the Riviera. Consequently, although there was no undue influence used, I was one of the very first female impersonators to appear on his show. I appeared with Tim Dunn, who happens to be a white male who does a fantastic impersonation of Dionne Warwick. Together we stole the show.

Montel Williams and me.

When things started getting too crazy for me to handle by myself, I decided I needed to hire a press agent. I was having a ball doing the talk show circuit and I wanted to make sure I would be aware of every opportunity available to me. Ergo, I hired Eric Kent. Almost immediately, he booked me on the **"Christina Show"** a Spanish show out of Miami, Florida.

On the set of the "Christina Show" in Florida.

Soon after, I once again made all the headlines. For the very first time ever, I, Frank Marino, was named:

"Showgirl of the Year in Las Vegas!"

This was obviously the first time a male had ever won this title. So again, I was invited back as a guest on the "Vicki Lawrence Show." This time they were doing a special taping in Las Vegas at the Desert Inn Hotel with Don Rickles as a co-host. Vicki Lawrence introduced me as the Showgirl of the Year in Las Vegas, but deliberately did not give my name. I came on stage dressed as a showgirl.

The outfit that won me "Showgirl of the Year."

I walked up to Mr. Rickles and planted a huge kiss on him. Mr. Rickles was smiling from ear to ear as he looked at me and asked, **"And what is your name pretty lady?"**

In the deepest voice I could muster I announced over a live mike, "Frank Marino!"

Mr. Rickles almost fell of his chair laughing. The shocked look on his face was worth a million dollars. Vicki Lawrence was in tears she was laughing so hard. **I don't think Mr. Rickles had ever been kissed by a man before!**

That little incident set the tempo for the rest of the show; Mr. Rickles and I bantered back and forth. We each told a few off-color jokes and made a lot of little innuendos. Basically, we all had a great time.

All in all, 1993 turned out to be a very good year. I was back in the press on a daily basis and I was appearing on almost every major television talk show on the air. **I was finally getting all the publicity and exposure that I yearned for throughout my career.**

The next show I agreed to make an appearance on was the **"Geraldo Show."** He was filming a show on "Teenagers and Plastic Surgery." I was asked to appear as a celebrity guest since over the years I had had so many surgeries.

So, I came on stage all made-up, I walked right over to Geraldo and planted this big kiss on him, just as I did to Don Rickles on the "Vicki Lawrence Show." Much to my surprise, when the show aired he had them edit it out! I couldn't believe it. Geraldo made sure it ended up on the cutting room floor. I still have no idea why, other than the fact that his reputation may have gotten tarnished!

Backstage with Geraldo
before I kissed him.

The man had on more makeup than I did and he was worried about his macho image.

After the Geraldo Show, my talk show appearances seemed to pick up even more momentum. I was in even greater demand than before and I was loving every minute of it.

I was then invited to appear on **"The Jenny Jones Show."** Jenny's background was similar to mine. Jenny also started out in Las Vegas. It wasn't that long ago she was a backup singer for Wayne Newton. Then she became a featured act in "Playboy Girls of Rock and Roll," a small cabaret show on the Strip. Later in her career she went on to Ed McMahon's Star Search and won! This gives me great hope that someday my dream of being a big television star might also come true.

She was extremely friendly. In fact, at one point during the show she mentioned on camera that she had been to see my show and thought it was fantastic. She went

The talk show twins.

on to mention that she was a fan of mine and envied the fact that I got to wear all those fabulous gowns and furs during the show. Jenny and I became great friends that day and I had become a regular on her show. She is an absolute doll and I would do her show anytime she wanted me there.

"A Current Affair" asked if I would be in a show they were doing called, "Keeping Me in Stitches," which ended up being a mini TV special on the life of Frank Marino and all the surgery I've had over the years. This particular episode had so much air play that once again all the tabloids wanted to do feature stories on me.

There were a lot of articles in magazines like Show Biz, Entertainment Today and The Globe. I was even interviewed by People Magazine eight different times. They couldn't get enough of me.

London Bridge is falling down.

My head was spinning with all the attention I had been generating. It soon started to have an adverse effect on my health. I was so exhausted from working six days a week at La Cage and then flying across country to do TV shows. I had to take a break so I packed my stuff and left for a well-deserved vacation in Europe.

Actually I think I freaked the English people out. **I don't think they have ever seen a Queen look this good.** I must say though, the highlight of that entire trip was stepping off the plane back here in America. I saw a lot of poverty and despair while I was traveling abroad, which only served to remind me **how lucky I was to call "America" my home!**

Soon after my return from Europe, I once again began receiving calls to make guest appearances on several other national talk shows. Having had plenty of time to relax and catch my breath, I decided to make my return to the talk shows by appearing on the **"Maury Povich Show"** in New York. As it turned out, my sister Sharon's nephew on her husband's side worked on the show. That's why the producer invited me to appear as a guest.

Crystal Woods, who impersonates Diana Ross in La Cage, accompanied me on this particular show. Maury had planned a beauty contest and the audience was supposed to guess who were the men and who were the women. There were five men and three women scheduled to appear as

Me with Maury Povich.
Hope Connie Chung doesn't get jealous.

guests. Chris Woods and I were both there as celebrity judges.

My entire family came into Manhattan and spent the afternoon with me after the show.

The next show on which I appeared was, in my opinion, the best. (Next to Joan Rivers, of course.) It was the **"Leeza"** show. She was doing a show called, "Dueling Divas." I loved the plot her producers came up with.

The basic plan was a face-off between the La Cage impersonators. There was Diana vs. Whoopi, Cher vs. Tina, Dolly vs. Reba, Michael vs. Janet, Judy vs. Liza, and so on and so forth. It sounded like something I would love to be a part of.

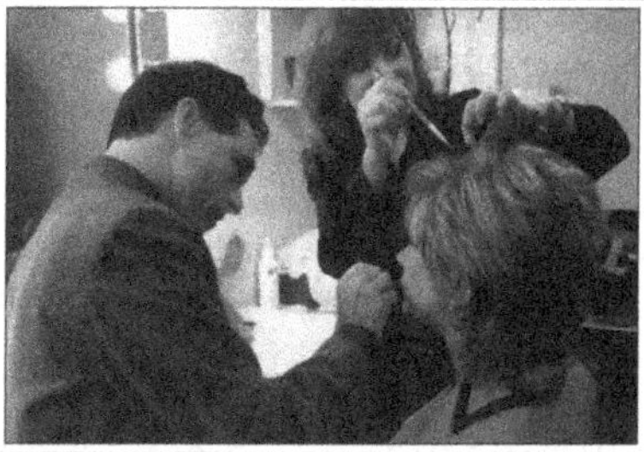

Keith Crary makes me up as Leeza.

There were going to be ten Female impersonators on the stage at the same time. The producers invited the entire cast of La Cage to appear. Once I had agreed, the producer decided to fill me in on the "cute idea" they had come up with. **Instead of my appearing as Joan Rivers as I normally would, they asked if I would play along with a spoof and appear as Leeza!**

This sounded like a fantastic idea. They supplied the outfit and Leeza's Emmy Award winning makeup artist, Keith Crary, to do my makeup. I was all for it. By show time, I had been transformed not into just a look-a-alike of Leeza, but an exact clone. The one flaw in the entire illusion was that I was slightly larger than Leeza.

I was totally convinced that I should have received an Emmy Award for my performance that day. Leeza was so wonderful, she even insisted that I keep the outfit I wore on the show. She really didn't have to go that far.

Seeing double. Will the real Leeza please stand up!

Leeza, if you are reading my book, call me and let's do another show!

I was addicted to the television talk show circuit. I couldn't seem to get on enough of them. I was a junkie just dying for my next fix. But my fix came in the form of lights, cameras and talk show hosts.

Doing the Leeza show had been, by far, such an absolutely pleasurable experience that all the other shows which followed appeared somewhat dim in the bright light of comparison.

As good an experience as Leeza's show was, **"The Rolanda Show"** portrayed the flipside of that coin and showed me just how poorly a talk show can actually be run. I have to tell you that it was the pinnacle of a nightmarish experience. Take my word for it! I guess I was so used to the plushness of all the other shows that I was expecting the same respect and treatment from the Rolanda staff. Instead I received the most repulsive, uncouth experience of a lifetime.

The show was supposed to be about practical jokes. **The title alone should have told me to avoid the situation.** Nevertheless, I was on a roll and wanted all the national exposure I could get. Besides, I was having such a great time. Until this show, anyway!

Rolonda's producers invited myself, as well as Carol Collier, who does a great job impersonating Whoopi Goldberg. Carol and I were to appear on stage as the actual stars. Then we were to melodramatically stage a mock argument with each other. **At the end of the squabble, we were instructed to pull each other's wigs off and reveal our true identities.** It was intended to be comical and the audience was expected to be stunned that we were actually men who performed as the female stars.

The very first indication of how this show was going to go down came the moment we arrived at the hotel. They sent us to the Lowes Hotel in Midtown Manhattan. This place must have gotten its name from its ratings. I was quite disappointed. **I felt this irresistible need to keep looking over my shoulder to make sure I wasn't about to get mugged!**

The second confirming clue came after we spent the night and had not even received as much as a phone call from the producers or any of the staff telling us where we had to go or when we had to be there. This had to be by far the most unorganized trashy production that I had ever encountered!

The final straw that literally broke the camel's back came when I had to sit in what they so incorrectly called "the green room" for four hours in a white silk suit. The room was a real ghetto. I shudder even now thinking about how filthy it was. **It made the basements and kitchens of those roach infested Discos I used to perform in look like the Taj Mahal.**

During the second hour, the staff did, however, come in and throw a cheese platter on the table as if we were a bunch of mice, or maybe it was there for the rats in the walls. Then when I asked to go to the restroom, I had to walk in a single file line just like a child in kindergarten, so the audience wouldn't see me.

By the end of the fourth hour, I was ready to walk out the door and keep on going. The only reason I didn't is because my mom was in the audience. **Thank goodness I was on during the first segment of the show.** I ended up spending less than five minutes in front of the camera after that four hour torture session.

By this time I was an animal. I was all but foaming at the mouth! I walked off the stage and asked for the limo to take me back to that awful hotel they had put me up in. It

This is where I would have put the photo of Rolanda had I stuck around long enough to take one with her.

came as no surprise when I was informed there was no limo available at that moment. **My stress level had reached its maximum.** I was so angry that I took a cab to the hotel.

I absolutely could not believe that a host as flawless and professional as Rolanda would have such a blatantly inefficient, unorganized, unprofessional staff. Rolanda, who is an incredible talent, should surround herself with people who know what the hell they're doing.

I was very down and felt a little uneasy about appearing on another show after the fiasco with Rolanda. Then one day I received a call from my good friend, Frank Hagen, who happens to be a producer on various shows. He asked me to appear on the new **"Danny Bonaduce Show."** I cautiously accepted.

For those of you who don't know Danny Bonaduce, he was the little red-headed kid named Danny on **"The Partridge Family!"** These days Danny is a very well-known radio Disc Jockey with his own radio talk show on the Loop in Chicago.

One of the main reasons I accepted the offer to appear on Danny's show was because I knew that Danny had once been arrested and charged with beating up a transvestite who he honestly believed to be a real woman. Therefore, I thought he and I would have a lot to talk about. The show's format was going to be similar to Johnny Carson's show.

I walked out on stage, went right over to Danny and gave him my famous big hello kiss, which each time resulted in a different reaction from the host. This time, the reaction was really cute. Danny looked up at me after I kissed him and said, **"I wasn't sure if I should kiss you or shake your hand."**

I looked at him and said, **"We all know you've had experience with people like me before!"** Danny blushed and very innocently asked, "What are you talking about?"

Coyly I responded, "You know what I mean," (remember, I was dressed as Joan Rivers). **"Talk Show Hosts!"** During the next segment, Danny and I talked as if we were old friends. The only flaw was that I forgot it was a Disney production. **Between the wise cracks and the jokes, my mouth kept getting me in trouble. At one point, there were so many bleeps and bloops it sounded more like someone trying to send a letter in Morse code rather than a talk show.**

On the Danny Show!

Two months later Danny was doing his radio show at the MGM Grand Hotel in Las Vegas and he was gracious enough to invite me on that show as well.

Thank goodness the **"Danny Bonaduce Show"** was such a positive experience. I don't know what it would have done to my self-esteem and my opinions regarding talk shows had it been another horrible situation like Rolanda.

While we are still on the topic of talk shows, one in particular I don't want to omit was the fiasco of **"The Gordon Elliot Show."** The topic of the show was "Drag," and the movie, **"To Wong Foo."** There were several other "Drag Stars" on the stage; Girlina was there, together with Jimmy James and a host of others. It was a national disaster. **The guests were walking off the stage left and right.** Girlina just up and disappeared in the middle of a segment, Jimmy James was so angry that he retaliated by insulting the entire staff.

Gordon Elliot sporting a new look with that beard.

The show was so run down and haphazardly thrown together, it had no chance of being a success.

I made the New York papers after that show.

Frank Marino, Star of the La Cage in Las Vegas Treated Like Bag Lady in New York!

My problem with the show was really very simple. I was asked to pay my own airfare with, of course, the promise that it would be reimbursed the moment I arrived at the show! I agreed, but when I arrived at the show, no one seemed to know anything about it. They passed the buck from one producer to another. Needless to say I got my money or I too would have walked off the stage.

During this time, between the good and the bad shows, I was asked to appear on the **"Sally Jessy Raphael Show."**

At Universal Studios as Fran Drescher filming the Sally Jessy Raphael Show.

She was filming a special show from Universal Studios. Although Sally felt that my appearing as Joan Rivers had been played out, she asked if I would appear as one of my other characters. **I told her I would love to appear as my newest character, Fran Drescher, also known as the "The Nanny" on her weekly television show.** Sally thought that was an excellent idea. As it turned out, the audience loved it and the show went great.

So, that's the dirt on all the talk shows.

I am sure I have left many of them out, but if I didn't, I probably wouldn't have enough pages in this book to fit them all on.

Recently, I've set my goals slightly higher. I'm now more interested in one day getting a role on a weekly television series, preferably a sitcom. Either that, or maybe one day:

**I'll be in the right place
at the right time and
I'll be the newest
discovery to hit
the big screen!**

14

A TV on TV

More and more I kept searching for ways to get myself on television. **I decided to try my hand at commercials.** I went on any and all auditions that would place me in front of the camera again. Before long, I had amassed an entire list of credits.

I did commercials for Bianca shoes, **(since I had been wearing high heels for so many years already, you might say I was a "shoe in" for the part)**, Celebrity Deli, the Junior League Foundation, Tiffany Dry Cleaners, Roland's Clothing Store and hundreds of other products. Each time I shot a commercial, I felt more and more comfortable in front of the camera.

Hollywood here I come.

Comedienne Glynis McCants. I'm one of her biggest fans.

Now I knew if I were ever going to be in sitcoms or movies, I needed to hire a Hollywood talent agent. This is the person who sends you out on auditions to get acting jobs. A good friend of mine, comedienne Glynis McCants, introduced me to her agent, Ralph, at the Gilla Roos Agency in Beverly Hills, California. When Ralph and I sat down to discuss my objectives, **I explained that I didn't want any of the normal "Drag Queen" stereotype roles,** like playing a prisoner or a prostitute. I wanted to do something different, funny, but still challenging.

During that spring, Ralph succeeded in obtaining for me an audition for a television show, although it is probably one of the things **I would most like to forget in my life.** I remember the details as if it happened yesterday. It was a Wednesday and as I had just returned from a one-day trip to Mardi Gras in New Orleans, I was completely exhausted and desperately needed some sleep.

There was a message on my answering machine that said, "Good news Frank, I got you an audition. The part looks good. I think you'll love it. The only catch is you have to be there to read for the director tomorrow afternoon."

What? The machine said the call had come in Wednesday morning. Ralph knew I worked on Thursdays. I thought about calling him back and asking if he had lost his mind. However, when I thought it out, I knew if I called the airlines before I left for work that day I could book a flight to California for early the next morning. I could meet with the director in the afternoon and still be back home in time for my show. I could always catch a few winks on the plane.

If you've got it, flaunt it.

I made it to the audition with about a half hour to spare Thursday afternoon. As soon as I got there, they handed me a script to look over. The girl pointed out the lines I was to read for the audition, then proceeded to give me a very brief synopsis of the story line.

The character I was reading for played three different characters in the story, two were men and one was a woman! **Talk about Sybil. I was used to the playing two people every night of the week, but three?** As I sat there looking over the part, I was amazed as well as amused at all the fifty cent words my character was supposed to use. Hey, I graduated from four years of college but I still couldn't pronounce half the words they wanted me to say, even if I used someone else's tongue. **Who wrote this thing, Einstein's nephew?**

The audition was basically over before it actually got started. I picked up my stuff and quickly left the studio. Exit stage left!

All the way home on the plane, I just couldn't help but laugh about how lousy I did at that audition. It had to be one of the most embarrassing experiences in my life. So, there went my first big chance of being in a television series, right out the window.

From there, I got lucky. It was on to bigger and better auditions. Since the Sally show, I've been infatuated with Fran Drescher.

Fran is as tough as Joan Rivers, only a lot sexier, which is exactly what attracted me to her character. What is it in New York that makes all these women so tough? The only differences between Fran and me are:

That's how I became the "Nanny" (me as Fran Drescher).

She is the Queen from Flushing, and I am the Queen of Las Vegas!

Anyway, my agent had booked me a nice part on the show, **"The Nanny."** For those of you who don't watch television, "The Nanny" is a weekly sitcom in which this big shot producer, Mr. Sheffield, hires a live-in nanny (Fran) to take care of his kids.

I went to the audition and everything went great. The episode I was hired for was centered around the fact that Joan Rivers had just had major plastic surgery. Therefore, the producer was hiding her out in his guest room so she could recuperate. No one was supposed to know she was there.

Suddenly, Fran finds out that the guest hiding out in the bedroom is a celebrity. She keeps trying to peek in to found out who it is. Didi Hanson (you know, the female Joan Rivers impersonator from the first Vicki Show) was going to play the part of Joan Rivers all bandaged up.

Through some very ingenious snooping, Fran discovers it is none other than Joan Rivers hiding there. She immediately calls all her friends and tells them she has Joan Rivers staying in her guest room. The entire situation snowballs out of control and before she knows what happened, the house and the entire yard are covered with reporters, television newscasters and her friends.

Her boss is outraged as he had promised Joan total secrecy as well as a comfortable place to recuperate. Fran takes control of the situation and insists she can take care of

Hanging out with Marvin always reminds me...a shake for breakfast, a shake for lunch and a sensible dinner.

everything without anyone ever finding out that Joan Rivers was there recovering from plastic surgery! Fran calls her cousin, Ira. **This is where I come in!** He impersonates Joan Rivers in a stage act. Isn't that a coincidence? She has him agree to dress as Joan and walk out the front door diverting all their attention, while the real Joan, still all bandaged up, sneaks out the back door. I was supposed to go in as a man, then come out as Joan Rivers when Didi, playing the real Joan, had safely escaped.

Well, everything was great. We were scheduled to shoot the episode in two weeks. One week before the show, the producers of the "The Nanny" saw a clip we had done previously of the "Leeza Show" on "Talk Soup," which is a cable show that highlights clips from the various talk shows during the week. That clip gave the producers the idea that it would be funnier to have big Cher, a comedy spoof that Marvin Nathan does in La Cage, rather than using me as Joan Rivers to play the part of the person having surgery.

I received the phone call explaining the changes in the script. **Needless to say, I was heart-broken because they had canceled me.** I really adore Fran and I am looking forward to working with her in the near future. Only this time, I'd like to do it dressed up as Fran, not Joan Rivers.

I think I'd make a good lifeguard, but don't think I'm getting my hair wet.

My next big television break came in January. David Hasselhoff, who you

Outside my trailer on the set of "Baywatch."

know has a nighttime show called **"Baywatch,"** came in and saw my act. He was working on a spin-off called **"Baywatch Nights."**

Instead of a lifeguard, David would be playing the part of a private detective whose office just happened to be located on the top floor of a nightclub. David fell in love with my act, as well as my show, and decided to do an episode of "Baywatch Nights" called, "Kind of a Drag."

I got a call from his producers and was asked to come in for an audition. I aced the audition and ended up working side by side in an episode where **David Hasselhoff and I were both dressed in drag! In fact, that photo of David and me dressed in drag got me in People magazine.** This photo was such a hit that even

David Hasselhoff gets in drag with me and co-star Angie Harmon.

Jay, just because Joan Rivers was banned from the show doesn't mean I have to be.

the European papers picked up the story.

I got more calls for interviews and auditions from that one picture than Michael Jackson got when he married Lisa Marie.

I hope to continue working in television and maybe someday break into movies. This way I would have the opportunity to appear on the "Tonight Show" with Jay Leno. He has done shows on every type of Las Vegas act, magicians, jugglers and showgirls. Once, he invited the La Cage dancers to be on the show and specifically told the producer to be sure that none of them were men in drag.

Maybe he has a prejudice against Female Impersonators. Maybe he thinks it's not a legitimate enough profession for the "Tonight Show" to discuss. The strange thing is: **I make more money than the president of the United States! How much more legitimate can you get?**

I decided I didn't want to become president when I realized it would mean moving into a smaller house in a bad neighborhood.

Dressing in female clothing is really nothing new. After all, if you look back through the years since the introduction of television, there have been many men who dressed in drag. Uncle Milty loved to dress as a female. Before him, "The Keystone Cops" had episodes where the escapees dressed as women to avoid being caught. Recently, even stars like Patrick Swayze and Wesley Snipes have done an entire movie in drag. Robin Williams did "Mrs. Doubtfire," and what about Dustin Hoffman in "Tootsie?"

Dressing in Drag is Entertainment.
Being Good and
Getting Paid for it is
Talent!

15

"Star Light, Star Bright! Here Are Some of The Stars I See at Night!"

During the fifteen years I've been performing, I have been fortunate enough to have met and had the opportunity to perform alongside some of the biggest and brightest stars in Hollywood. Here are just a few of my favorites.

One of the big fans of La Cage is **Neil Sedaka**. I know you all remember "Laughter in the Rain!" Neil would regularly hang out backstage, then we'd frequently go out for a late night dinner or an early breakfast. I'll never forget during the Joan Rivers lawsuit, Neil was playing on the same bill with Joan at Caesars Palace. Neil told me to meet him at the Riviera Hotel instead of me

Neil Sedaka and me.

That's what friends are for.
Me with Ms. Dionne Warwick.

going to Caesars so I wouldn't be in an awkward position if I saw Joan.

We decided to go to a nightclub and, would you believe it, when I pulled up to the nightclub who was standing right there in the valet parking? None other than Joan Rivers herself. So, there we were, Neil, Joan and myself. I think all of us just about died. Joan was very polite and the funny thing is we ended up spending the rest of the night together.

Another regular at La Cage was **Ms. Dionne Warwick.** Once, Dionne gave Crystal Woods a beautiful beaded gown as a gift to wear in the show. When Dionne was the host of "Solid Gold" she would often invite us to L.A. to watch the taping of the show and whenever she was performing at the Golden Nugget in Las Vegas she would invite the entire cast to come as her guests to see her perform.

Sammy Davis Jr. would also bring his entire family and all of his friends to see our show. It was not uncommon to look out into the audience and see Sammy with an entire entourage of people sitting in one of the booths.

Me with "The Candy Man,"
Sammy Davis Jr.

There was one time in particular when he invited me to his show that I will always remember. I was sitting out in the audience, when right in the middle of his act Sammy stopped the show and introduced me. This was the first time I had been introduced by any star while watching their performances. I was taken aback and honored by his acknowledgement.

While Sammy may be gone now, he will never be forgotten.

Hello, Carol.

One of my all-time favorite celebrities has to be **Carol Channing.** She is definitely one of the most recognized celebrities in the world. I remember she came to see Ron Raymond impersonate her. After the show she gave each of us fake Cracker Jack diamond rings. She must have bought a thousand boxes in order to get that many matching rings. Either that, or maybe she ransacked a gumball machine. While she was backstage, we spent some time playing with all my shoes and the different wigs. Carol is an absolute doll.

With Phyllis Diller at her 75th birthday party.

Debbie Reynolds shows me around her new hotel in Las Vegas.

Phyllis Diller! Now there's a name from the past. I was invited to her seventy-fifth birthday party held in Las Vegas at the **Debbie Reynolds Hotel**. If you want to talk about a "Drag Queen's Dream," Phyllis Diller wins that title hands down. She has positively no competition.

This woman has the best skin in the world. In person, she looks half her age. Although I must admit, I hear she's had more surgery than I have. She was joking with me and said at one point her face had so many wrinkles she had to screw her hat on.

Backstage with Rip Taylor after my show.

Speaking of the Debbie Reynolds Hotel, **Rip Taylor** just happened to be a part owner of that hotel. I had the pleasure of doing a television special on "A Current Affair" with Rip not long ago. This man is one of the craziest people I have ever met. He can turn any gathering into a full-blown party in a matter of minutes. I love being in his presence as you are guaranteed to have a great time. Rip Taylor could have made Scrooge laugh.

Me with five-time Grammy Award winner Whitney Houston.

One of the most nerve-racking but thrilling experiences I've had was the night **Whitney Houston** came to see the show. I was a nervous wreck the entire evening. Whitney was sitting at the foot of the stage; I wanted everything to be perfect, and thankfully, the show was flawless. Everyone was at their peak and each performer outdid the one before them.

Whitney gave everyone a standing ovation for their performance. After the show we were standing around talking when Sarah called. She had just arrived in Vegas and she and my Aunt Lucy were in the hotel lobby. I invited both of them upstairs to meet Whitney. I could have died when she said, "No thanks, I'm too tired. You come down and meet me in the lobby."

I was so embarrassed as Whitney was standing at my side during the entire conversation. How was I supposed to tell her my mother was too tired to come and meet a celebrity of her status? Whitney handled it very graciously. She just smiled and said, "I have a mom and she gets tired, too." What a great lady.

Good golly, it's Dolly!

One time when Dolly Parton and Kenny Rogers were performing at The Mirage Hotel in Las Vegas, my good friend, Joey Skilbred, who happens to be a fabulous artist **(as well as the designer of the Frank Marino doll),** had painted a portrait of Dolly and invited me to accompany him when he delivered it to her backstage. Having admired Dolly for so long, I quickly agreed to tag along. She had just gone

Designer Joey Skilbred made me feel like a living doll.

through a total make-over. She had lost all that extra weight and she looked even more fantastic than usual. Dolly was so impressed with the painting that she autographed a picture of herself and gave it to Joey. I have to tell you, even up close Dolly is a very beautiful woman.

Some years ago, I was fortunate enough to have the opportunity to see **Whoopi Goldberg** perform in Las Vegas. Talk about a talented lady. She is definitely one of the best stand-up comics in the business. She invited my entire family backstage after the show. **Jerry Lewis** was also in the audience that evening and I introduced myself. He later contacted me to appear on his telethon. I, of course, said yes and have been appearing ever since. Talk about being in the right place at the right time!

Whoopi! I met an Academy Award winner.

Another time I was with two of my

Singing with the supreme
Miss Diana Ross.

best friends, Michael Cetta and Michael Buonpastore, and we went to see Diana Ross at Caesars Palace. After the show, we decided to go shopping in the Caesars Palace Forum Shops. I was looking at shoes when I saw a sales clerk locking the doors. Little did I know that **Diana Ross** was also in the store. Evidently when she goes into a store to buy something, they lock the doors so a crowd doesn't gather. You can imagine how excited I was when I discovered I was locked in the shoe store with **Diana Ross!**

With my two friends,
Mike and Mike.

Me and Suzanne Somers
after her show in Las Vegas.
Trust me, the Thigh Master really works.

I asked her if she would have a picture taken with me. After all the years of impersonating her, now I was shopping in the same store she was. Talk about having your heart stop!

I could go on and on about all the stars I have rubbed elbows with over the years. There are people like **Suzanne Somers**, who every time the two of us are in the same room we tell Thigh Master jokes.

Me with my dear friend, Shirley MacLaine. I was also friends with her in a past life.

I can't forget to mention **Rosie O'Donnell**, an old friend of mine whom I had the pleasure of meeting way back when she was a comedienne at the Improv, which was also at the Riviera Hotel. Just recently I had the pleasure of running into Rosie on an airplane. She had just had her daytime talk show debut, and has since become one of the biggest sensations to hit the air waves in a long time. Who knows, maybe she'll let me be the first Drag Queen ever to appear on her show.

Me with the star of the Moulin Rouge,
LaToya Jackson.

Out on the town with Gloria Estefan.

Over the years, I've also made friends with **LaToya Jackson,** whom I got the chance to see perform at the Moulin Rouge while I was in Paris. People often belittle her talent, but I'm here to tell you that if you stop comparing her to her brother Michael, you'd see she is also very talented in her own right.

One of the funniest times I ever spent with a celebrity was when **Gloria Estefan** played at the Las Vegas Hilton. Of course, the crowds were going crazy because she was such a big star. I desperately wanted to meet her and luckily, I was invited backstage. Gloria asked me where was there to go in this town for the night life. The only problem was, anywhere she went she would be recognized, so I lent her one of my short black wigs and we went to the Discos and nightclubs. No one knew who she was. In fact, one of the nightclubs ID'ed her. I think if the crowd had known it was Gloria Estefan they would have died.

To this day, I get a thrill out of meeting other famous people. It's still as exciting for me as when I first met Joan Rivers.

16

A Friend and a Lover!

We all have our idea of the perfect soul mate. We all yearn to find that ideal person to make our lives complete and to fill the void of coming home to an empty house night after night. We want that someone who can share our dreams, understand our needs, be there to help us should we fall, and celebrate with us when we succeed.

There have been a couple of times in my life when I was convinced that I had found that perfect someone. Unfortunately, they had other ideas!

Mr. Shannon (Alex) Schechter.

My definition of the perfect partner is basically very simple. My lover would have to be very understanding; my schedule is very demanding and hard to contend with. They would have to accept me for who I am and what I do. I can be temperamental and **I can be a bitch to live with.** In fact, there are some days when even I wish I could move out on myself. My lover would also have to be good looking! Someone I could be proud to walk alongside and who would be equally as proud to walk alongside me.

I do have a current partner, Shannon Schechter (he now goes by his middle name, Alex). One night, while in my car driving home from work, we were both stopped next to each other at a red light. We kept glancing at one another and when the light turned green, we took off but he kept glancing back at me. **The next thing I knew, he was being pulled over by a cop.**

It wasn't until a week later on July fourth that a mutual friend of ours, Ken Schneider, (one of my best friends and a new friend of Shannon's), introduced us. I later learned the reason he was stopped was because he was driving without a valid license plate. I was surprised to discover that Shannon, along with several family members, had recently been in to see La Cage. We talked for hours that night and eventually I invited him to join me for an early breakfast. We continued to talk long after breakfast. We exchanged phone numbers and agreed to get together again soon for dinner and a movie.

The day Ken introduced me to Shannon.

A couple of days went by and finally he called. We agreed to have dinner and then go to see Bette Midler's new movie, "Hocus Pocus."

Shannon and I at the La Cage 10 year anniversary kickoff party.

Actually, our first "date" was rather comical. Instead of going to a fancy restaurant where I normally would have taken any dinner guest, **I took Shannon to McDonald's.** While we were standing in line, he turned to me and timidly said, "Who pays for dinner?"

I couldn't resist the open invitation. I turned, looked into his eyes, and with a straight face announced, **"Whoever I'm with pays!"** For the briefest of moments I could see the look of relief cross his face that we were indeed at McDonald's and not some fancy restaurant. However, when I reached for my wallet, he smiled and asked if I took all my dates to McDonald's. "Only on the first date," I said, struggling to hold back a chuckle. I felt comfortable talking to him, and it was easy for each of us to discuss our expectations openly and honestly.

Shannon and I spent a lot of time together. We do have a lot in common and we have a lot of the same interests. He had just graduated from college with an advertising degree and I felt it was important for him to pursue his career.

His interests were advertising and journalism, which were a great advantage to me, because from time to time we work together on various projects (like this book which has kept us both up until 6 a.m. every morning for the last six months). We basically have a fairly conventional relationship.

Of course, like any couple there are the famous family issues. Pretty much both of our families accept our relationship. His family occasionally has a hard time dealing with certain situations. On one occasion when his mother was having company, she put all the pictures he had of me in his bedroom in a dresser drawer so the relatives would not get suspicious. I later joked with his mom and asked her **if that was her climbing up the side of the Riviera Hotel trying to take my billboard down.**

I think each day that passes makes it easier for everyone to understand. Nonetheless, we have always been

Eat your hearts out, Siegfried and Roy.

invited to family lunches and gatherings as a pair. We vacation together, we do almost everything as a couple, although as of yet we don't live together.

I actually love him too much to subject him to my moodiness on a twenty-four hour, seven day a week basis. However, if I asked him to, I am sure he would.

The mock wedding photo Shannon and I took for Ten Percent magazine.

There are still a few small kinks in our relationship that need to be worked out. **He is slightly jealous over the attention I get from fans and admirers.** He has a very possessive nature and I am the complete opposite. I am not the jealous type. Don't they say something about opposites attracting? I think part of his insecurity arises from the fact that we cannot openly display our affection for one another.

I, as a rule, am not usually open about my sexuality, or for that matter my sexual preferences. Don't misunderstand my statement. If somebody has the balls to ask me, I will tell them the truth.

"I just don't flaunt my choices."

17

Closets are for Clothes!

Today elegance lies really within the nature of the person, rather than what they could possibly wear. **In a sense, this has always been true but never challenged...**

When I first began impersonating famous women, I would simply borrow clothes from my sister's closet. Then when I began making money performing, I started buying a few off-the-rack dresses. As my career progressed even further, I eventually had many of my outfits custom made. Before long, my closets contained **hundreds of gowns which ranged in price from $1 to $10,000 apiece.** Through

My dressing room closet in Las Vegas.

the years I have amassed a wardrobe that even the **Princess of Wales would envy.**

I'll never forget the first gown that was ever custom made for me. Would you believe, it was from a Simplicity pattern? My dear and close friend, Anabelle Dimizzio, made it for me. The gown was absolutely gorgeous and fit like a glove. I'm sure this was the first time she had ever been asked to make a dress for a man.

Later in my career after I moved to Vegas, I met Daniel Storey. Right there in the living room of his house, **he created the most beautiful beaded gowns that I had ever seen**. It wasn't long after that that I made a name for myself on the Las Vegas Strip as a clothes horse. In 1993, I even had the honor of winning the **Review Journal's Best Dressed Las Vegan Award.**

The LAS VEGAS REVIEW-JOURNAL 12th ANNUAL

BEST of LAS VEGAS

Frank Marino

has been selected by the Las Vegas Review-Journal staff as the

Best Dressed-Las Vegan

of Las Vegas, Nevada.

1993

Sherman R. Frederick, Publisher

March 7, 1993

Date

LAS VEGAS REVIEW-JOURNAL

Daniel Storey also went on to build a name for himself as a costume designer with his partner, Bob Michaels.

Today, the names on the gowns that hang in my closet read like the "who's who" of fashion. Names such as Mary McFadden, Todd Oldham, Coco Chanel, Gianni Versace, Vera Wang and the list goes on and on - not to mention all the Stephen Yearicks and Bob Mackies hanging in there.

Each year, I select a designer to make a special line of clothes for me. This year I've selected Charles Mezrahi at Clair's Collection. So far, he has created some of the most theatrical couture evening gowns I have ever seen.

Remember though, buying a beautiful designer gown is the easiest part of the total look. **It's actually fitting into a size seven that's the hard part.**

I'm sure you've all seen those gorgeous, toned bodies on television; you know the ones with the string bikinis. If you ask me, it makes them all look like they're flossing their asses! However, the truth is, we've all wanted to look like those so-called goddesses on the TV screen at one time or another.

Watch your hands,
Mr. Yearick, I'm a lady!

Listen to me, I've tried every diet under the sun. The Beverly Hills Diet, the Grapefruit Diet, **and one time I even tried a diet where you eat all your meals naked in front of a mirror. This really works, but I found that fancier restaurants really don't go for it!**

No, seriously, I now have a new savior in life. Her name is Susan Powter.

This is my ball dress.
I have two of them.

You know the blond diet guru with the crop top haircut. Her theory is: eat as much as you want, but watch your fat intake, try to keep it at 30% of your total daily calories instead of the 45-50% which most Americans indulge in. This, along with any home exercise video like the Jane Fonda workout tapes, will help burn those unwanted calories you've eaten during the day. The pounds will drop like crazy and your entire body will become toned. All this without missing a meal. You'll soon find you look great in any outfit you decide to wear.

It's not who you are,
it's what you wear.

However, the clothes alone do not make the woman. There are so many other necessities that have to be added to enhance the package.

Anyone for won-ton soup?

Shoes! One of my favorite accessories. Some women love handbags. Liz Taylor loves her diamonds. Me, I love my shoes. I have hundreds and hundreds of pairs - not your typical shoes either. I'm referring to shoes designed by the greats like Charles Jordan, Stuart Weitzman, Kenneth Cole, Giorgio Armani, Victor Costa. Again, the list goes on and on. **These, my friends, are shoes!**

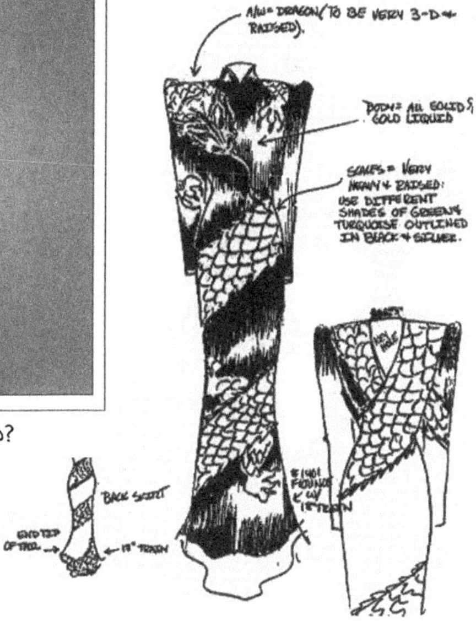

Of course, we all want the things that people see on us to sparkle and glitter, but there are also things we wear that people won't see. Unfortunately in my business, one such necessity is pantyhose. Most of the time I wear Donna Karan brand, sheer to waist opaque skin tone support hose. Only because, **while I want to look naked, I don't want to feel it.** I need them to be strong and these look great, feel great, and last forever.

As I have said before, I change gowns seventeen times per show. With all those quick as lightning changes, I don't want to chance getting a run in my stockings.

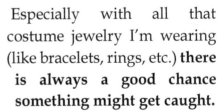

Especially with all that costume jewelry I'm wearing (like bracelets, rings, etc.) **there is always a good chance something might get caught.**

I get all my show jewelry from Carol Daniels, my friend in Florida. She is probably the most exotic

Carol Daniels and I. Can you tell who the drag queen is?

woman I have ever met. She travels the world and picks up the most unique pieces for me. Over the years I have become so obsessed with my accessories that I often find myself spending thousands of dollars on costume jewelry.

I constantly alternate my wardrobe on a regular basis. I hate to be out of fashion or style. When something starts to get old or worn out, I go to the local Goodwill shop and donate the garments.

You've come a long way baby.

It's a strange feeling when you donate clothes to places like that because you never know where they're going to end up next.

I just know that there's a bag lady somewhere in the world wearing my red Oleg Cassini gown. I just hope she was able to find the right color shoes to match!

18

A Decade of Drag

There was a soft knock on my dressing room door, then those old familiar words: **"Five minutes Mr. Marino!"**

Although I had heard those same words millions of times in the past, tonight they carried a special meaning! Tonight's performance was the pinnacle of my career. **It was my ten year anniversary at the Riviera Hotel in Las Vegas** where I've been entertaining audiences three shows a night, six nights a week, fifty weeks a year and I'm here to tell you, I loved every waking moment of it.

The Queen of the Las Vegas Strip.

As I glanced silently into the mirror, I thought to myself, at the tender age of thirty-one life couldn't be better. My name was up in neon lights, on huge billboards

Norbert, Marlene and I toast to our ten year anniversary.

and cab backs throughout Las Vegas. I was the star of "La Cage," the world's most famous female impersonation revue. **I had just signed a new multi-million dollar contract guaranteeing my appearances on stage through the beginning of the twenty-first century!** Not too shabby for an orphaned boy from Brooklyn, New York.

My only regret in life is that my parents did not live long enough to see me become a star. I've always felt that getting to the top was the easy part, but staying there is the hard part. **That's why I was extremely honored when, after ten years of hard work, I was still chosen as the best female impersonator in Las Vegas.**

1995 TOURIST TOP CHOICE
LAS VEGAS ENTERTAINMENT AWARDS
BEST FEMALE IMPERSONATOR
Frank Marino
PUBLISHER, LAS VEGAS ENTERTAINMENT
LAS ENTERTAINMENT TODAY The Magazine VEGAS

I must admit, being a celebrity in Las Vegas comes with some perks. No more waiting in long lines at any of the popular restaurants. My guests and I are always assured the

On the Carol and Marilyn show.

best table in the house. **Las Vegas is a great town to be famous in.** If you're a celebrity, everybody wants to know you. They will cater to your every need, but I try to live by my motto: **"It's nice to be important, but it's even more important to be nice!"**

One of my biggest fans is Lillian White who has actually seen my show more than three hundred times. Recently, we were invited to Los Angeles as guests on the **"Carol and Marilyn"** morning show to talk about her fascination with La Cage.

The mayor of Las Vegas, Jan Jones, and me at a fund-raiser.

When I appear on these shows, people often ask me, "Frank, why do you dress up in women's clothing?"

Hello, gorgeous...
A spoof on Babs.

Together again, Joan and I in '95.

My standard answer is **"CASH..."** The truth of the matter is because **"I'm a natural born entertainer." I love making people happy!**

Despite the fact that Joan Rivers sued me in 1986, I still have great respect for her and admire her ability to make others feel good. All in all, Joan and I have remained close friends and she is still a large part of my act. **However, I can be any character I want to be, except, of course, Barbra Streisand.** After nine surgeries, my nose is much too slender to pull that one off!

I'll tell you though, doing an impersonation of a comedian can sometimes be difficult, especially when you have to be the person **laughing on the outside when you're sometimes crying on the inside**. I have to smile even when I'm sad.

I also have the great responsibility of making

thousands of people a night laugh and forget their troubles as they watch my show.

I guess if you want to be a star, you must also pay the price. That twenty-plus minutes I spend doing my monologue can make or break the way an audience perceives the rest of the show. If I come off as being the slightest bit depressed, I can bring the whole room down. As long as I'm upbeat and cheerful, the audience will respond accordingly.

Most people in Las Vegas think they know Frank Marino, but I don't think anybody really knows me.

I'm very cautious in the selection of people I choose to associate with. I've been used by people because of who I am and it's taken me a long time to find the true friends I now have. These are friends that are not just around because I am star.

I do, in fact, receive lots of fan mail. There's even a Frank Marino fan club, where people can write to me and find out lots of personal details. If you are interested in joining my fan club, simply write to:

The Frank Marino Fan Club
9041 Sandy Shore Drive
Las Vegas, Nevada 89117

A long time ago, I took some of Joan Rivers' advice. She once told me, **"Without the fans, you are nothing. As quickly as they made you, they can break you."** That's why I feel it's important to answer all my fan mail personally.

Although my life got off to what some people might call a rocky start, I'm proud of the way it's turned out so far. I was raised by a wonderful, loving, caring family who allowed me to follow my dreams and all my goals in life. I was given every opportunity to be whatever I wanted to be.

My entire family at Christmas. From left to right, Sarah, Aunt Lucy, Shannon, Nadine, Damien, Ace, Alan, Toni, Scott, Sharon and Samantha (I took the photo).

If I couldn't be a female impersonator anymore, I don't know what I'd want to be.

There is a lot of work that goes into each and every performance that I do. I constantly need to change my act and keep it modern. This is extremely difficult, but I do it

My #1 fan, Lillian White, and I check the stage before a benefit show for AIDS.

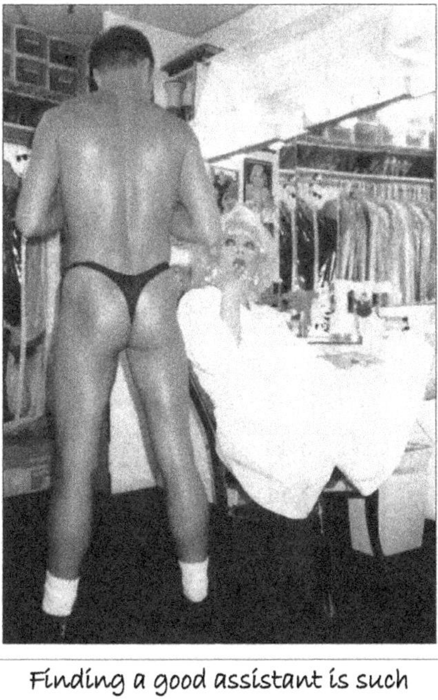

Finding a good assistant is such a pain in the ass.

and this is why I've lasted for ten years while other headliners have come and gone.

The hardest part for me is coming up with current comedy material to freshen up my routines and keep them up to date, but I reap the rewards of my grueling labors with each and every audience as they applaud the illusions I've created for them.

My 1995 Calendar.
The dog looks better than I do. Bitch!

I want everyone to realize that entrainment is a give-and-take type business. I make sure that when I'm not doing live performances or appearing on talk shows, I donate all my free time to charities and benefits. One of my favorite charities is **AMFAR**, which is dedicated to **AIDS Research**. In 1995, I donated a portion of the proceeds from my national calendar through the Landmark Corporation to help fund their efforts.

I also travel around the country to appear at Pride festivals and do benefit shows to raise money for local charities.

For me, it's the best feeling in the world to be able to help out someone in need.

What makes a man a man?

I think the most unfortunate thing in my life is that I've lived out almost all my fantasies. It's sad but true. I've just about done it all.

My remaining goals involve getting the rest of the world to know who Frank Marino is.

I want to be the best at whatever I decide to do. Thanks to my determination, I think I have a pretty good shot at it!

I don't know where I'm going,
but I know from where I've come.
No matter where life takes me,
I'll always cherish
where I've been.

19

Author's Notes 1997

If anyone ever asks me what the hardest thing I ever had to do in **my life** was, it wouldn't be walking in **high heels** or even learning to apply **makeup** correctly, my answer would have to be writing this **book**.

Nobody ever warned me of all the sleepless nights and twenty-four hour work days that would go into an **autobiography**. But I'm sure glad I did it.

The first cookbook I ever wrote and I don't know how I got away with it. I'm so bad in the kitchen I have a stove that flushes!

After celebrating my ten year anniversary at **La Cage**, I decided the time was right for me to tell the world my story.

I spent a whole year remembering and reliving my entire life, even the painful parts that I have tried to block out and forget forever. I never realized how **painful** remembering those times in my life would be.

I realize now that it's the pain and the heartache in our lives that gives each of us the strength to achieve our **goals**. Fortunately for me, the good times have always outweighed the bad times.

Remember, the key to unlocking your **dreams** is in your heart. So if everything you do is with **love**, all your dreams will come true.

All in all, I've had a **fabulous** life thus far. I've been to many exciting places and met many fascinating people. I'm happy to say that I've done more in this short period of time than others have done in an entire lifetime. But for me, that's not an excuse to just sit back and relax. I feel I must always go forward and face each new **challenge** head on.

**Life is like a roller coaster.
What lies ahead I cannot predict,
but I'll tell you this, if it's anything
like the past ten years,
it's going to be an
exciting ride!**

20

Drags to Riches (2014 Update)

Wow! It's been a while since we talked. The last fifteen years have been wild. Now I'm Las Vegas's longest running headliner and the producer and star of my own show named **Frank Marino's Divas, Las Vegas!** I can't believe how much has happened. Let me tell you… **but not all of it.** I'm just going to brush up on the highlights because the rest is already being written for **my new book, Drags to Riches** coming out next year!

After writing my first book, His Majesty, the Queen, I got so depressed (going over my parents' deaths and the hard times of my childhood). I took an antidepressant called Paxil and thought it was great until I won the jackpot of Paxil side effects and lost my voice. Only no one knew it! Here I was slurring my words all over the place and they just thought I was drunk (totally humiliating since I'm not a drinker at all).

About that same time, my producer went nuts. He told the whole town that I was expendable! **This Queen doesn't know how to be expendable!** He turned the cast of La Cage against me. He locked me in a tiny dressing room and said, "Perform!" I felt like Shirley Temple in the Little Princess.

Who's expendable now?

Talk about falling down off my highest perch. Here I'd done Miss Congeniality II, I'd gotten a star on the Strip, and La Cage and I were riding high on the publicity of our 20th Anniversary on the Strip and my producer has to ruin it all by trying to put me in my place. One lawsuit, 36 months, and me hanging up my hat as ambassador for La Cage and what do you know?

La Cage closes.

The Millionaire Matchmaker, Tony and Tina's Wedding, and Toddlers and Tiaras are just a few of the television shows I've been on. Alex and I travelled a bit together, we broke up, we got back together and now we're engaged! We have a brand new child, okay dog, Cherié. I'll tell you all about it but not here. It's too much! **I need a whole new book to go into all that!**

Once I was out from under the thumb of my old producer, I hit the streets with my own show. After six months of pounding the pavement, I got a show with the largest entertainment company in the world, Caesars Entertainment, but I didn't stop there. I'm my own boss now. I didn't take "no" for an answer. I don't just have one show, I've got several! I don't just have one star on the Strip, I have two, a key to the city and a street named after me.

Once again, I'm back on top and nobody's going to keep me down this time. I'm talking to you now as the longest running headliner of Las Vegas, and the owner of the most successful and biggest drag show in the world, **Frank Marino's Divas, Las Vegas** at the all new LINQ Hotel and Casino. I celebrated my 50th birthday in the famous Elvis suite at the Hilton. My new mission is to meet every celebrity that I've ever impersonated. These are just a few of the highlights. I'll tell you all about it with lots of pictures in Drags to Riches releasing next year.

For more about Frank Marino or Divas, visit us on the web at:

Frank Marino

f /FrankMarinoFanPage
@TheQueenOfVegas
@TheQueenOfVegas
FrankMarino.com
FrankMarinosDivas
#TheQueenofVegas

Divas Show

f /DivasLV
@DivasLV
@DivasLasVegas
FrankMarinosDivas.com
#DivasLasVegas